WHAT'S COOKING
chinese

Jenny Stacey

DP
DEMPSEY
PARR

First published in Great Britain in 1998 by
Dempsey Parr
13 Whiteladies Road
Clifton
Bristol
BS8 1PB

ISBN: 1-84084-182-6

Printed in Italy

Produced by Haldane Mason, London

Acknowledgements
Art Director: Ron Samuels
Editorial Director: Sydney Francis
Editorial Consultant: Christopher Fagg
Managing Editor: Jo-Anne Cox
Editor: Linda A. Doeser
Design: Digital Artworks Partnership Ltd
Photography: Andrew Sydenham
Home Economist: Kathryn Hawkins
Home Economist's Assistant: Eliza Baird

Note
Cup measurements in this book are for American cups.
Tablespoons are assumed to be 15 ml. Unless otherwise stated,
milk is assumed to be full fat, eggs are medium
and pepper is freshly ground black pepper.

Contents

Introduction

In the West we tend to talk about Chinese cooking as a generalization, as though it were the same throughout China. In fact, China is a vast country, with a range of topography and climates that produce distinct regional differences. The availability of ingredients varies from region to region and as the Chinese use fresh ingredients in the majority of their cooking, dishes are influenced by availability.

This book, contains recipes that are popular in both China and the West. Dishes from Szechuan in the West, Canton in the South, Beijing in the North and Shanghai in the East offer a wonderful array of different flavours and cooking methods. This book uses the up-to-date cooking methods of China, which produce colourful healthy dishes using simple ingredients, combining colour, texture and flavours well. The dishes included in this book range from hot and spicy to delicate flavours using fish and vegetables, with a mid-range of sweet-and-sour dishes, rice, noodles and a small section of desserts.

One of the most important features of Chinese cooking is texture. Vegetables should remain crisp, and rice and noodles should be treated like pasta and retain their 'bite' after cooking. Ingredients such as tofu (bean curd) are used for texture, even though they have little flavour in themselves. Bamboo shoots, a common ingredient, are included purely for texture.

Although the Chinese make use of regional, fresh foods, they also use dried foodstuffs in their recipes, in particular mushrooms, tofu (bean curd), noodles and spices. These were first developed to preserve foods, but are now widely used.

REGIONAL VARIATIONS

In Beijing, the cold northerly climate strongly affects the cuisine. There is quite a variety in this region which has inherited influences from the Mandarin courts, and there was also some Manchurian and Mongolian input. Wheat is more popular than rice and many noodle, pancake and dumpling recipes originate from this area. They also glaze, barbecue (grill) and spit-roast many of their meats. Sauces are robust and rich, using many spices, soy sauce and garlic. Lamb is the most popular meat in this area as a result of the Mongolian influence.

Cantonese cooking in the South is entirely different. Here, stir-frying produces rich, inventive and colourful food. Traders and travellers have influenced the cuisine and the sub-tropical climate, perfect for fruit growing, has meant that many savoury dishes include fruit, as well as fish and seafood. Very little meat is eaten in the south, although they are famed for their 'red' cooking, whereby foods are braised in soy sauce to give a red colour. Soy is used extensively here in the thick sauces which are characteristic, and rice is always included in a meal.

In the East, more starch is eaten and considerably more fat is used. Rice is served as an accompaniment or for stuffings. Rice wine is produced and used in abundance, perfectly complementing the range of fish and seafood caught along the coastline. The people of Shanghai have a sweet tooth and savoury dishes are much sweeter from this region.

Szechuan cooking from the West is hearty and spicy. They use many chillies and spices, producing hot-and-sour, piquant flavours. Pickles feature in the regional cooking, and the foods are traditionally drier, but combine many flavours. Sauces are kept to a minimum, even in stir-fries.

COOKING METHODS

There are several cooking methods used in this book, although very little special equipment is required. The Chinese tend to combine a couple of cooking methods in one dish, such as steaming and then frying, or frying and roasting.

Steaming is widely used in Chinese cookery. Traditionally bamboo steamers are used, so that a whole meal may be cooked in one stack of bamboo racks. The rice is usually placed in the bottom and different dishes stacked on top, those taking the longest to cook being placed at the bottom. If you do not have a steamer, invert a heatproof plate in a large saucepan and cover it with a lid or foil. Boiling water is added to the steamer, to cover one third of the depth of the dish. This water may need topping up during cooking, although many of the dishes cook very quickly. Steaming is a very healthy method of cooking, not using any fat, and it traps the flavours of the dish.

Stir-frying is done in a wok that must be heated before use. Foods of similar size (all small) are stirred constantly, so that as they come into contact with the wok, they cook quickly. Sometimes foods are cooked in batches and removed. This is to preserve flavours. The dishes are always brought together in the wok at the end of cooking and may have sauces added during or at the end of the cooking time, depending on the region from which they originated. Peanut oil is usually used for stir-frying, but vegetable oil may be used in its place.

Deep-frying is also done in the wok, which uses less oil than a deep-fryer. The shape of the wok allows oil to drain from the food into the centre of the wok. The foods are often marinated first or coated in a light batter. **Quick-frying** is also used, whereby foods are either fried on one side (used for noodles) and not turned or turned once and sliced for serving.

INGREDIENTS

Most of the recipes in this book use ingredients readily available in western supermarkets, but more traditional options have been suggested where appropriate. It is worth making a trip to a Chinese supermarket or specialist food shop for high-quality soy sauce and some of the other slightly more obscure ingredients, but the recipes will all work very well and be equally delicious without them.

Bamboo shoots *These are added purely for texture, as they have very little flavour. Available in cans, they are a common ingredient in Chinese cooking.*

Beansprouts *These are mung bean shoots, which are very nutritious, containing many vitamins. They add crunch to a recipe and are widely available. Do not overcook them, as they wilt and do not add texture to the dish.*

Black beans *These are soy beans and are very salty. They can be bought and crushed with salt and then rinsed or used in the form of a ready-made sauce for convenience.*

Chinese beans *These long beans may be eaten whole and are very tender. French (green) beans may also be used.*

Chinese five spice powder *An aromatic blend of cinnamon, cloves, star anise, fennel and brown peppercorns. It is often used in marinades.*

Chinese leaves *A light green leaf with a sweet flavour. It can be found readily in most supermarkets.*

Coriander (cilantro) *Also known as Chinese parsley, this has a strong, pungent flavour and resembles parsley in appearance only. Use it sparingly to avoid overpowering dishes.*

Hoisin sauce *A dark brown, sweet, thick sauce that is widely available. It is made from spices, soy sauce, garlic and chilli and is often served as a dipping sauce.*

Lychees *These are worth buying fresh, as they are easy to prepare. Inside the inedible skin is a fragrant white fruit. Lychees are available canned and are a classic ingredient.*

Mango *Choose a ripe mango and delight in the sweet, scented flesh. If a mango is underripe when bought, leave it in a sunny place for a few days before using.*

Noodles *The Chinese use several varieties of noodle. You will probably find it easier to use the readily available dried varieties, such as egg noodles, which are yellow, rice stick noodles, which are white and very fine, or transparent noodles, which are opaque when dry and turn transparent on cooking. These may not be easy to find, and cellophane or rice noodles may be used instead.*

Oyster sauce *Readily available, this sauce is made from oysters, salt, seasonings and cornflour (cornstarch) and is brown in colour.*

Pak choi *Also known as Chinese cabbage, this is available in some supermarkets. It has a mild, slightly bitter flavour.*

Rice vinegar *This has a mild, sweet taste that is quite delicate. It is available in some supermarkets and is well worth obtaining. If it is not available, use cider vinegar.*

Rice wine *This is similar to dry sherry in colour, alcohol content and smell, but it is worth buying rice wine for its distinctive flavour.*

Sesame oil *This is made from roasted sesame seeds and has an intense flavour. It burns easily and is therefore added right at the end of cooking for flavour, and is not used for frying.*

Soy sauce *This is widely available, but it is worth buying a good grade of sauce. It is produced in both light and dark varieties – the former is used with fish and vegetables for a lighter colour and flavour, while the latter, being darker, richer, saltier and more intense, is used as a dipping sauce or with strongly flavoured meats.*

Star anise *This is an eight-pointed, star-shaped pod with a strong aniseed flavour. The spice is also available ground. If a pod is added to a dish, it should be removed before serving.*

Szechuan pepper *This is quite hot and spicy and should be used sparingly. It is red in colour and is readily available.*

Tofu (bean curd) *This soya bean paste is available in several forms. The cake variety, which is soft and spongy and a white-grey colour, is used in this book. It is very bland, but adds texture to dishes and is perfect for absorbing all the other flavours in the dish.*

Water chestnuts *These are flat and round and can usually only be purchased in cans, already peeled. They add a delicious crunch to dishes and have a sweet flavour.*

Yellow beans *Again a soy bean and very salty. Yellow bean sauce has been used in this book, and it is suggested you purchase a good variety that is chunky rather than smooth.*

Soups & Starters

In China soups are not usually served at the beginning of a meal but between courses to clear the palate. It is also quite common for Chinese families to serve a large tureen of clear soup at the same time as the other dishes. The soups in this chapter bring a whole range of flavours and textures to the table. There are thicker soups, thin clear consommés and those topped with wontons for effect and flavour. These soups can be eaten as a lunch or snack on their own – whatever your preference, they all taste delicious!

The starters in this chapter are a combination of old favourites and traditional Chinese dishes, and there is sure to be something to suit every occasion. One of the advantages of these dishes is that they can be prepared and cooked in advance. Instead of serving the starters individually, try serving a small portion of each together as an assorted hors d'oeuvres. Remember not to have more than one of the same type of food – the ingredients should be chosen for their harmony and balance in colour, aroma, flavour and texture.

Clear Chicken & Egg Soup

This tasty chicken soup has the addition of poached eggs, making it both delicious and filling. Use fresh, home-made chicken stock for a better flavour.

Serves 4

INGREDIENTS

1 tsp salt
1 tbsp rice wine vinegar
4 eggs
850 ml/1¹/2 pints/3³/4 cups
   chicken stock

1 leek, sliced
125 g/4¹/2 oz broccoli florets
125 g/4¹/2 oz/1 cup shredded
   cooked chicken
2 open-cap mushrooms, sliced

1 tbsp dry sherry
dash of chilli sauce
chilli powder, to garnish

1 Bring a large saucepan of water to the boil and add the salt and rice wine vinegar. Reduce the heat so that it is just simmering and carefully break the eggs into the water, one at a time. Poach the eggs for 1 minute. Remove the poached eggs with a slotted spoon and set aside.

2 Bring the chicken stock to the boil in a separate pan and add the leek, broccoli, chicken, mushrooms and sherry and season with chilli sauce to taste. Cook for 10–15 minutes.

3 Add the poached eggs to the soup and cook for a further 2 minutes. Carefully transfer the soup and poached eggs to 4 individual soup bowls. Dust with a little chilli powder to garnish and serve immediately.

VARIATION

You could substitute 125 g/4½ oz fresh or canned crabmeat or the same quantity of fresh or frozen cooked prawns (shrimp) for the chicken, if desired.

COOK'S TIP

You could use 4 dried Chinese mushrooms, rehydrated according to the packet instructions, instead of the open-cap mushrooms, if you prefer.

Curried Chicken & Sweetcorn (Corn) Soup

Tender cooked chicken strips and baby corn cobs are the main flavours in this delicious clear soup, with just a hint of ginger.

Serves 4

INGREDIENTS

175 g/6 oz can sweetcorn
  (corn), drained
850 ml/1¹/₂ pints/3³/₄ cups
  chicken stock

350 g/12 oz cooked, lean chicken, cut
  into strips
16 baby corn cobs
1 tsp Chinese curry powder

1-cm/¹/₂-inch piece fresh root ginger
  (ginger root), grated
3 tbsp light soy sauce
2 tbsp chopped chives

1 Place the canned sweetcorn (corn) in a food processor, together with 150 ml/¹/₄ pint/²/₃ cup of the chicken stock and process untilthe mixture forms a smooth purée.

2 Pass the sweetcorn purée through a fine sieve, pressing with the back of a spoon to remove any husks.

3 Pour the remaining chicken stock into a large saucepan and add the strips of cooked chicken. Stir in the sweetcorn (corn) purée.

4 Add the baby corn cobs and bring the soup to the boil. Boil the soup for 10 minutes.

5 Add the curry powder, grated ginger and soy sauce and cook for a further 10–15 minutes. Stir in the chopped chives.

6 Transfer the soup to warm soup bowls and serve immediately.

COOK'S TIP

Prepare the soup up to 24 hours in advance without adding the chicken, cool, cover and store in the refrigerator. Add the chicken and heat the soup through thoroughly before serving.

Hot & Sour Soup

This well-known soup from Peking is easy to make and very filling. It is often eaten as a meal on its own and should be served before a light menu if it is offered as an appetizer.

Serves 4

INGREDIENTS

2 tbsp cornflour (cornstarch)
4 tbsp water
2 tbsp light soy sauce
3 tbsp rice wine vinegar
1/2 tsp ground black pepper

1 small fresh red chilli,
   finely chopped
1 egg
2 tbsp vegetable oil
1 onion, chopped

850 ml/1 1/2 pints/3 3/4 cups chicken
   or beef consommé
1 open-cap mushroom, sliced
50 g/1 3/4 oz skinless chicken breast,
   cut into very thin strips
1 tsp sesame oil

1 Blend the cornflour (cornstarch) with the water to form a smooth paste. Add the soy sauce, rice wine vinegar, pepper and chilli and mix together well.

2 Break the egg into a separate bowl and beat well.

3 Heat the oil in a preheated wok and fry the onion for 1–2 minutes.

4 Stir in the consommé, mushroom and chicken and bring to the boil. Cook for about 15 minutes or until the chicken is tender.

5 Pour the cornflour (cornstarch) mixture into the soup and cook, stirring constantly, until it thickens.

6 As you are stirring, gradually drizzle the egg into the soup, to create threads of egg.

7 Sprinkle with the sesame oil and serve immediately.

COOK'S TIP

Make sure that the egg is poured in very slowly and that you stir continuously to create threads of egg and not large pieces.

Peking Duck Soup

This is a hearty and robustly flavoured soup, containing pieces of duck and vegetables cooked in a rich stock.

Serves 4

INGREDIENTS

125 g/4¹/₂ oz lean duck breast meat
225 g/8 oz Chinese leaves (cabbage)
850 ml/1¹/₂ pints/3³/₄ cups chicken
   or duck stock

1 tbsp dry sherry or rice wine
1 tbsp light soy sauce
2 garlic cloves, crushed
pinch of ground star anise

1 tbsp sesame seeds
1 tsp sesame oil
1 tbsp chopped fresh parsley

1 Remove the skin from the duck breast and finely dice the flesh.

2 Using a sharp knife, shred the Chinese leaves (cabbage).

3 Put the stock in a large saucepan and bring to the boil.

4 Add the sherry or rice wine, soy sauce, diced duck meat and shredded Chinese leaves and stir to mix thoroughly. Reduce the heat and leave to simmer gently for 15 minutes.

5 Stir in the garlic and star anise and cook over a low heat for a further 10–15 minutes, or until the duck is tender.

6 Meanwhile, dry-fry the sesame seeds in a preheated, heavy-based frying pan (skillet) or wok, stirring constantly.

7 Remove the sesame seeds from the pan and stir them into the soup, together with the sesame oil and parsley.

8 Spoon the soup into warm bowls and serve immediately.

COOK'S TIP

If Chinese leaves (cabbage) are unavailable, use leafy green cabbage instead. You may wish to adjust the quantity to taste, as Western cabbage has a stronger flavour and odour than Chinese leaves (cabbage).

Beef & Vegetable Noodle Soup

Thin strips of beef are marinated in soy sauce and garlic to form the basis of this delicious soup. Served with noodles, it is both filling and delicious.

Serves 4

INGREDIENTS

225 g/8 oz lean beef
1 garlic clove, crushed
2 spring onions (scallions), chopped
3 tbsp soy sauce
1 tsp sesame oil

225 g/8 oz egg noodles
850 ml/1$\frac{1}{2}$ pints/3$\frac{3}{4}$ cups beef stock
3 baby corn cobs, sliced
$\frac{1}{2}$ leek, shredded

125 g/4$\frac{1}{2}$ oz broccoli, cut into florets (flowerets)
pinch of chilli powder

1 Using a sharp knife, cut the beef into thin strips and place them in a shallow glass bowl.

2 Add the garlic, spring onions (scallions), soy sauce and sesame oil and mix together well, turning the beef to coat. Cover and leave to marinate in the refrigerator for 30 minutes.

3 Cook the noodles in a saucepan of boiling water for 3–4 minutes. Drain the noodles thoroughly and set aside until required.

4 Put the beef stock in a large saucepan and bring to the boil.

5 Add the beef, together with the marinade, the baby corn, leek and broccoli. Cover and leave to simmer over a low heat for 7–10 minutes, or until the beef and vegetables are tender and cooked through.

6 Stir in the noodles and chilli powder and cook for a further 2–3 minutes. Transfer to bowls and serve immediately.

COOK'S TIP

Vary the vegetables used, or use those to hand. If preferred, use a few drops of chilli sauce instead of chilli powder, but remember it is very hot!

Lamb & Rice Soup

This is a very filling soup, as it contains rice and tender pieces of lamb.
Serve before a light main course.

Serves 4

INGREDIENTS

150 g/5½ oz lean lamb
50 g/1¾ oz/¼ cup rice
850 ml/1½ pints/3¾ cups
   lamb stock

1 leek, sliced
1 garlic clove, thinly sliced
2 tsp light soy sauce
1 tsp rice wine vinegar

1 medium open-cap mushroom,
   thinly sliced
salt

1 Using a sharp knife, trim any fat from the lamb and cut the meat into thin strips. Set aside until required.

2 Bring a large pan of lightly salted water to the boil and add the rice. Bring back to the boil, stir once, reduce the heat and cook for 10–15 minutes, until tender. Drain, rinse under cold running water, drain again and set aside until required.

3 Meanwhile, put the lamb stock in a large saucepan and bring to the boil.

4 Add the lamb strips, leek, garlic, soy sauce and rice wine vinegar to the stock in the pan. Reduce the heat, cover and leave to simmer for 10 minutes, or until the lamb is tender and cooked through.

5 Add the mushroom slices and the rice to the pan and cook for a further 2–3 minutes, or until the mushroom is completely cooked through.

6 Ladle the soup into 4 individual warmed soup bowls and serve immediately.

COOK'S TIP

Use a few dried Chinese mushrooms, rehydrated according to the packet instructions and chopped, as an alternative to the open-cap mushroom. Add the Chinese mushrooms with the lamb in step 4.

Fish Soup with Wontons

This soup is topped with small wontons filled with prawns (shrimp),
making it both very tasty and satisfying.

Serves 4

INGREDIENTS

125 g/4¹/₂ oz large, cooked, peeled
  prawns (shrimp)
1 tsp chopped chives
1 small garlic clove, finely chopped

1 tbsp vegetable oil
12 wonton wrappers
1 small egg, beaten
850 ml/1¹/₂ pints/3³/₄ cups fish stock

175 g/6 oz white fish fillet, diced
dash of chilli sauce
sliced fresh red chilli and chives,
  to garnish

1 Roughly chop a quarter of the prawns (shrimp) and mix together with the chopped chives and garlic.

2 Heat the oil in a preheated wok and stir-fry the prawn (shrimp) mixture for 1–2 minutes. Remove from the heat and set aside to cool completely.

3 Spread out the wonton wrappers on a work surface (counter). Spoon a little of the prawn (shrimp) filling into the centre of each wrapper. Brush the edges of the wrappers with beaten egg and press the edges together, scrunching them to form a 'moneybag' shape. Set aside while you are preparing the soup.

4 Pour the fish stock into a large saucepan and bring to the boil. Add the diced white fish and the remaining prawns (shrimp) and cook for 5 minutes.

5 Season to taste with the chilli sauce. Add the wontons and cook for a further 5 minutes. Spoon into warmed serving bowls, garnish with sliced red chilli and chives and serve immediately.

VARIATION

Replace the prawns (shrimp) with cooked crabmeat for an alternative flavour.

Crab & Ginger Soup

*Two classic ingredients in Chinese cooking are blended together
in this recipe for a special soup.*

Serves 4

INGREDIENTS

1 carrot, chopped
1 leek, chopped
1 bay leaf
850 ml/1^1/2 pints/3^3/4 cups fish stock

2 medium-sized cooked crabs
2.5-cm/1-inch piece fresh root ginger
(ginger root), grated
1 tsp light soy sauce

^{1}/2 tsp ground star anise
salt and pepper

1 Put the carrot, leek, bay leaf and stock into a large pan and bring to the boil. Reduce the heat, cover and leave to simmer for about 10 minutes, or until the vegetables are nearly tender.

2 Meanwhile, remove all of the meat from the cooked crabs. Break off the claws, break the joints and remove the meat (you may require a fork or skewer for this). Add the crabmeat to the saucepan of fish stock.

3 Add the ginger, soy sauce and star anise to the fish stock and bring to the boil. Leave to simmer for about 10 minutes, or until the vegetables are tender and the crab is heated through. Season to taste with salt and pepper.

4 Ladle the soup into warmed serving bowls and garnish with crab claws. Serve at once.

COOK'S TIP

*If fresh crabmeat is unavailable,
use drained canned
crabmeat or thawed frozen
crabmeat instead.*

COOK'S TIP

*To prepare cooked crab, loosen the
meat from the shell by banging the
back of the underside with a
clenched fist. Stand the crab on its
edge with the shell towards you.
Force the shell from the body with
your thumbs. Twist off the legs and
claws and remove the meat. Twist
off the tail and discard. Remove and
discard the gills from each side of the
body. Cut the body in half along
the centre and remove all of the
meat. Scoop the brown meat from
the shell with a spoon.*

Shrimp Dumpling Soup

These small dumplings filled with shrimp and pork may be made slightly larger and served as dim sum *on their own, if you prefer.*

Serves 4

INGREDIENTS

DUMPLINGS:
150 g/5$^1/_2$ oz/1$^5/_8$ cups plain (all-purpose) flour
50 ml/2 fl oz/$^1/_4$ cup boiling water
25 ml/1 fl oz/$^1/_8$ cup cold water
1$^1/_2$ tsp vegetable oil

FILLING:
125 g/4$^1/_2$ oz minced (ground) pork
125 g/4$^1/_2$ oz cooked peeled shrimp, chopped
50 g/1$^3/_4$ oz canned water chestnuts, drained, rinsed and chopped
1 celery stick, chopped
1 tsp cornflour (cornstarch)

1 tbsp sesame oil
1 tbsp light soy sauce

SOUP:
850 ml/1$^1/_2$ pints/3$^3/_4$ cups fish stock
50 g/1$^3/_4$ oz cellophane noodles
1 tbsp dry sherry
chopped chives, to garnish

1 To make the dumplings, mix together the flour, boiling water, cold water and oil in a bowl until a pliable dough is formed.

2 Knead the dough on a lightly floured surface for 5 minutes. Cut the dough into 16 equal-sized pieces.

3 Roll the dough pieces into rounds about 7.5 cm/3 inches in diameter.

4 Mix the filling ingredients together in a large bowl.

5 Spoon a little of the filling mixture into the centre of each round. Bring the edges of the dough together, scrunching them up to form a 'moneybag' shape. Twist to seal.

6 Pour the fish stock into a large saucepan and bring to the boil.

7 Add the cellophane noodles, dumplings and dry sherry to the pan and cook for 4–5 minutes, until the noodles and dumplings are tender. Garnish with chopped chives and serve immediately.

COOK'S TIP

Wonton wrappers may be used instead of the dumpling dough if time is short.

Chinese Cabbage Soup

This is a piquant soup, which is slightly sweet-and-sour in flavour. Chinese cabbage is cooked in a vegetable broth with sugar, vinegar and chilli and served as a hearty meal or appetizer.

Serves 4

INGREDIENTS

450 g/1 lb pak choi
600 ml/1 pint/2¹/₂ cups
   vegetable stock
1 tbsp rice wine vinegar

1 tbsp light soy sauce
1 tbsp caster (superfine) sugar
1 tbsp dry sherry
1 fresh red chilli, thinly sliced

1 tbsp cornflour (cornstarch)
2 tbsp water

1 Using a sharp knife, trim the stems of the pak choi and shred the leaves.

2 Heat the stock in a large saucepan. Add the pak choi and cook for 10–15 minutes.

3 Mix the rice wine vinegar, soy sauce, sugar and sherry together. Add this mixture to the stock, together with the sliced chilli. Bring to the boil, lower the heat and cook for 2–3 minutes.

4 Blend the cornflour (cornstarch) with the water to form a smooth paste. Gradually stir the cornflour (cornstarch) mixture into the soup. Cook, stirring constantly, until it thickens. Cook for a further 4–5 minutes. Ladle the soup into individual warm serving bowls and serve immediately.

VARIATION

Boil about 2 tbsp rice in lightly salted water until tender. Drain and spoon into the base of the soup bowls. Ladle the soup over the rice and serve immediately.

COOK'S TIP

Pak choi, *also known as* bok choi *or spoon cabbage, has long, white leaf stalks and fleshy, spoon-shaped, shiny green leaves. There are a number of varieties available, which differ mainly in size rather than flavour.*

Spring Rolls

This classic Chinese dish is very popular in the West.
Serve hot or chilled with a soy sauce or hoisin dip.

Serves 4

INGREDIENTS

175 g/6 oz cooked pork, chopped
75 g/2³/4 oz cooked chicken, chopped
1 tsp light soy sauce
1 tsp light brown sugar
1 tsp sesame oil
1 tsp vegetable oil
225 g/8 oz beansprouts

25 g/1 oz canned bamboo shoots,
    drained, rinsed and chopped
1 green (bell) pepper, seeded and chopped
2 spring onions (scallions), sliced
1 tsp cornflour (cornstarch)
2 tsp water
vegetable oil, for deep-frying

SKINS:
125 g/4¹/2 oz/1¹/8 cups plain (all-
    purpose) flour
5 tbsp cornflour (cornstarch)
450 ml/16 fl oz/2 cups water
3 tbsp vegetable oil

1 Mix the pork, chicken, soy, sugar and sesame oil. Cover and marinate for 30 minutes.

2 Heat the vegetable oil in a wok. Add the beansprouts, bamboo shoots, (bell) pepper and spring onions (scallions) and stir-fry for 2–3 minutes. Add the meat and the marinade to the wok and stir-fry for 2–3 minutes.

3 Blend the cornflour (cornstarch) with the water

and stir the mixture into the wok. Set aside to cool completely.

4 To make the skins, mix the flour and cornflour (cornstarch) and gradually stir in the water, to make a smooth batter.

5 Heat a small, oiled frying pan (skillet). Swirl one-eighth of the batter over the base and cook for 2–3 minutes. Repeat with the remaining batter. Cover with a damp tea towel (dish cloth).

6 Spread out the skins and spoon one-eighth of the filling along the centre of each. Brush the edges with water and fold in the sides, then roll up.

7 Heat the oil for deep-frying in a wok to 180°C/350°F. Cook the spring rolls, in batches, for 2–3 minutes, or until golden and crisp. Remove from the oil with a slotted spoon and drain on absorbent kitchen paper (paper towels). Serve immediately.

Pork Dim Sum

*These small steamed parcels are traditionally served as an appetizer
and are very adaptable to your favourite fillings.*

Serves 4

INGREDIENTS

400 g/14 oz minced (ground) pork
2 spring onions (scallions), chopped
50 g/1³/4 oz canned bamboo shoots,
    drained, rinsed and chopped

1 tbsp light soy sauce
1 tbsp dry sherry
2 tsp sesame oil
2 tsp caster (superfine) sugar

1 egg white, lightly beaten
4¹/2 tsp cornflour (cornstarch)
24 wonton wrappers

1 Mix together the minced (ground) pork, spring onions (scallions), bamboo shoots, soy sauce, dry sherry, sesame oil, sugar and beaten egg white in a bowl until well combined.

2 Stir in the cornflour (cornstarch), mixing well.

3 Spread out the wonton wrappers on a work surface (counter). Place a spoonful of the pork and vegetable mixture in the centre of each wonton wrapper and lightly brush the edges of the wrappers with water.

4 Bring the sides of the wrappers together in the centre of the filling, pinching firmly together.

5 Line a steamer with a clean, damp tea towel (dish cloth) and arrange the wontons inside. Cover and steam for 5–7 minutes, until cooked through. Serve.

COOK'S TIP

Bamboo steamers are designed to rest on the sloping sides of a wok above the water. They are available in a range of sizes.

VARIATION

Use prawns (shrimp), minced (ground) chicken or crabmeat for the filling, with other vegetables, such as chopped carrot, and flavourings, such as chilli or ginger, if you prefer.

Crispy Crab Wontons

*These delicious wontons are a superb appetizer. Deep-fried until crisp
and golden, they are delicious with a chilli dipping sauce.*

Serves 4

INGREDIENTS

175 g/6 oz white crabmeat, flaked
50 g/1³/4 oz canned water chestnuts,
   drained, rinsed and chopped
1 small fresh red chilli, chopped

1 spring onion (scallion), chopped
1 tbsp cornflour (cornstarch)
1 tsp dry sherry
1 tsp light soy sauce

¹/2 tsp lime juice
24 wonton wrappers
vegetable oil, for deep-frying
sliced lime, to garnish

1 To make the filling, mix
together the crabmeat, water
chestnuts, chilli, spring onion
(scallion), cornflour (cornstarch),
sherry, soy sauce and lime juice.

2 Spread out the wonton
wrappers on a work surface
(counter) and spoon one portion
of the filling into the centre of
each wonton wrapper.

3 Dampen the edges of the
wonton wrappers with a
little water and fold them in half
to form triangles. Fold the two
pointed ends in towards the

centre, moisten with a little
water to secure and then pinch
together to seal.

4 Heat the oil for deep-frying
in a wok or deep-fryer to
180°C–190°C/350°F–375°F, or
until a cube of bread browns in
30 seconds. Fry the wontons, in
batches, for 2–3 minutes, until
golden brown and crisp. Remove
the wontons from the oil and leave
to drain on kitchen paper (paper
towels).

5 Serve the wontons hot,
garnished with slices of lime.

COOK'S TIP

*Wonton wrappers, available from
Chinese supermarkets, are paper-
thin squares made from wheat-flour
and egg. They can be easily
damaged, so handle them carefully.
Make sure that the wontons are
sealed well and secured before deep-
frying to prevent the filling coming
out and the wontons unwrapping.*

Pancake Rolls

This is another classic dim sum *dish which is adaptable to almost any filling of your choice. Here the traditional mixture of pork and pak choi is used.*

Serves 4

INGREDIENTS

4 tsp vegetable oil
1–2 garlic cloves, crushed
225 g/8 oz minced (ground) pork
225/8 oz pak choi, shredded

4¹/₂ tsp light soy sauce
¹/₂ tsp sesame oil
8 spring roll skins, 25 cm/10 inches
   square, thawed if frozen

oil, for deep-frying
chilli sauce (see Cook's Tip, below),
   to serve

1 Heat the vegetable oil in a preheated wok. Add the garlic and stir-fry for 30 seconds. Add the pork and stir-fry for 2–3 minutes, until just becoming lightly coloured.

2 Add the shredded pak choi, soy sauce and sesame oil to the wok and stir-fry for 2–3 minutes. Remove from the heat and set aside to cool.

3 Spread out the spring roll skins on a work surface (counter) and spoon 2 tablespoons of the pork mixture along one edge of each. Roll the skin over once and fold in the sides. Roll up completely to make a sausage shape, brushing the edges with a little water to seal. If you have time, set the pancake rolls aside for 10 minutes to seal firmly.

4 Heat the oil for deep-frying in a wok until almost smoking. Reduce the heat slightly and fry the pancake rolls, in batches if necessary, for 3–4 minutes, until golden brown. Remove from the oil with a slotted spoon and drain on kitchen paper (paper towels). Serve with chilli sauce.

COOK'S TIP

To make chilli sauce, heat 60 g/ 2 oz/¼ cup caster (superfine) sugar, 50 ml/2 fl oz/¼ cup rice vinegar and 2 tbsp water in a small saucepan, stirring until the sugar has dissolved. Bring the mixture to the boil and boil rapidly until a light syrup forms. Remove the pan from the heat and stir in 2 finely chopped, fresh red chillies. Leave the sauce to cool before serving. If you prefer a milder dipping sauce, deseed the chillies before chopping them.

Sesame Prawn (Shrimp) Toasts

These small toasts are easy to prepare and are one of the most popular Chinese appetizers in the West.
Make sure you serve plenty of them as they are very tasty!

Serves 4

INGREDIENTS

225 g/8 oz cooked, peeled
    prawns (shrimp)
1 spring onion (scallion)
$^{1}/_{4}$ tsp salt

1 tsp light soy sauce
1 tbsp cornflour (cornstarch)
1 egg white, beaten

3 thin slices white bread,
    crusts removed
4 tbsp sesame seeds
vegetable oil, for deep-frying

1 Put the prawns (shrimp) and spring onion (scallion) in a food processor and process until finely minced (ground). Alternatively, chop them very finely. Transfer to a bowl and stir in the salt, soy sauce, cornflour (cornstarch) and egg white.

2 Spread the mixture on to one side of each slice of bread. Spread the sesame seeds on top of the mixture, pressing down well.

3 Cut each slice into four equal triangles or strips.

4 Heat the oil for deep-frying in a wok until almost smoking. Carefully place the triangles in the oil, coated side down, and cook for 2–3 minutes, until golden brown. Remove with a slotted spoon and drain on kitchen paper (paper towels). Serve hot.

VARIATION

If wished, you could add ½ tsp very finely chopped fresh root ginger and 1 tsp Chinese rice wine to the prawn (shrimp) mixture at the end of step 1.

COOK'S TIP

Fry the triangles in two batches, keeping the first batch warm while you cook the second, to prevent them from sticking together and overcooking.

Sweet & Sour Battered Prawns (Shrimp)

These delicious prawns (shrimp) are marinated in a soy sauce mixture before being coated in a light batter, fried and served with a delicious sweet-and-sour dip.

Serves 4

INGREDIENTS

16 large raw prawns (shrimp), peeled
1 tsp grated fresh root ginger
1 garlic clove, crushed
2 spring onions (scallions), sliced
2 tbsp dry sherry
2 tsp sesame oil
1 tbsp light soy sauce
vegetable oil, for deep-frying
shredded spring onion (scallion),
　to garnish

BATTER:
4 egg whites
4 tbsp cornflour (cornstarch)
2 tbsp plain (all-purpose) flour

SAUCE:
2 tbsp tomato purée (tomato paste)
3 tbsp white wine vinegar
4 tsp light soy sauce
2 tbsp lemon juice

3 tbsp light brown sugar
1 green (bell) pepper, seeded and cut
　into thin matchsticks
$1/2$ tsp chilli sauce
300 ml/$1/2$ pint/$1^{1}/4$ cups vegetable
　stock
2 tsp cornflour (cornstarch)

1 Using tweezers, devein the prawns (shrimp), then flatten them with a large knife.

2 Place the prawns (shrimp) in a dish and add the ginger, garlic, spring onions (scallions), sherry, sesame oil and soy. Cover and marinate for 30 minutes.

3 Make the batter by beating the egg whites until thick. Fold in the cornflour (cornstarch) and flour to form a light batter.

4 Place all of the sauce ingredients in a pan and bring to the boil. Reduce the heat and leave to simmer for 10 minutes.

5 Remove the prawns (shrimp) from the marinade and dip them into the batter to coat.

6 Heat the oil until almost smoking. Reduce the heat and fry the prawns (shrimp) for 3–4 minutes, until crisp and golden brown. Serve with the sauce.

Prawn (Shrimp) Rice Paper Parcels

These special rice paper wrappers are available in Chinese supermarkets and health shops. Do not use the rice paper sold for making cakes.

Serves 4

INGREDIENTS

1 egg white
2 tsp cornflour (cornstarch)
2 tsp dry sherry
1 tsp caster (superfine) sugar
2 tsp hoisin sauce

225 g/8 oz peeled, cooked
  prawns (shrimp)
4 spring onions (scallions), sliced
25 g/1 oz canned water chestnuts,
  drained, rinsed and chopped

8 Chinese rice paper wrappers
vegetable oil, for deep-frying
hoisin sauce or plum sauce,
  to serve

1 Lightly beat the egg white, then mix in the cornflour (cornstarch), dry sherry, sugar and hoisin sauce. Add the prawns (shrimp), sliced spring onions (scallions) and water chestnuts, mixing thoroughly.

2 Soften the rice papers by dipping them in a bowl of water one at a time. Spread them out on a work surface (counter).

3 Spoon a little of the prawn (shrimp) mixture into the centre of each rice paper and wrap the paper around the filling to make a secure parcel.

4 Heat the oil in a wok until it is almost smoking. Reduce the heat slightly, add the parcels, in batches if necessary, and deep-fry for 4–5 minutes, until crisp. Remove from the oil with a slotted spoon and drain on absorbent kitchen paper (paper towels).

5 Transfer the parcels to a warmed serving dish and serve immediately with a little hoisin or plum sauce.

COOK'S TIP

Use this filling inside wonton wrappers (see page 30) if the rice paper wrappers are unavailable.

Crab Ravioli

These small parcels are made from wonton wrappers, filled with mixed vegetables and crabmeat and cooked to perfection for a melt-in-the-mouth starter.

Serves 4

INGREDIENTS

450 g/1 lb crabmeat (fresh or canned and drained)
1/2 red (bell) pepper, seeded and finely diced
125 g/4 1/2 oz Chinese leaves (cabbage), shredded

25 g/1 oz beansprouts, roughly chopped
1 tbsp light soy sauce
1 tsp lime juice
16 wonton wrappers
1 small egg, beaten

2 tbsp peanut oil
1 tsp sesame oil
salt and pepper

1 Mix together the crabmeat, (bell) pepper, Chinese leaves (cabbage), beansprouts, soy sauce and lime juice in a bowl. Season and leave to stand for 15 minutes, stirring occasionally.

2 Spread out the wonton wrappers on a work surface (counter). Spoon a little of the crabmeat mixture into the centre of each wrapper, dividing it equally between them.

3 Brush the edges of the wrappers with the beaten egg and fold in half, pushing out any air. Press the edges together with your fingers to seal tightly.

4 Heat the peanut oil in a preheated wok or frying pan (skillet). Fry the ravioli, in batches, for 3–4 minutes, turning until browned. Remove with a slotted spoon and drain on paper towels.

5 Heat the remaining filling in the wok or frying pan (skillet) over a gentle heat until hot. Serve the ravioli with the hot filling and sprinkled with sesame oil.

COOK'S TIP

Make sure that the edges of the ravioli are sealed well and that all of the air is pressed out to prevent them from opening during cooking.

Spare Ribs

Another classic favourite in Chinese restaurants, these sticky ribs are best eaten with your fingers.

Serves 4

INGREDIENTS

900 g/2 lb pork spare ribs
2 tbsp dark soy sauce
3 tbsp hoisin sauce

1 tbsp Chinese rice wine or dry sherry
pinch of Chinese five spice powder
2 tsp dark brown sugar

1/4 tsp chilli sauce
2 garlic cloves, crushed
coriander (cilantro) sprigs, to garnish
(optional)

1 Cut the spare ribs into separate pieces if they are joined together. If desired, you can chop them into 5 cm/2-inch lengths, using a cleaver.

2 Mix together the soy sauce, hoisin sauce, Chinese rice wine or sherry, Chinese five spice powder, dark brown sugar, chilli sauce and garlic in a large bowl.

3 Place the ribs in a shallow dish and pour the mixture over them, turning to coat them well. Cover and marinate in the refrigerator, turning the ribs from time to time, for at least 1 hour.

4 Remove the ribs from the marinade and arrange them in a single layer on a wire rack placed over a roasting tin (pan) half filled with warm water. Brush with the marinade, reserving the remainder.

5 Cook in a preheated oven, at 180°C/350°F/Gas Mark 4, for 30 minutes. Remove the roasting tin (pan) from the oven and turn the ribs over. Brush with the remaining marinade and return to the oven for a further 30 minutes, or until cooked through. Transfer to a warmed serving dish, garnish with the coriander (cilantro) sprigs (if using) and serve immediately.

COOK'S TIP

Add more hot water to the roasting tin (pan) during cooking if required. Do not allow it to dry out as the water steams the ribs and aids in their cooking.

Honeyed Chicken Wings

*Chicken wings are ideal for a starter as they are small and
perfect for eating with the fingers.*

Serves 4

INGREDIENTS

2 tbsp peanut oil
450 g/1 lb chicken wings
2 tbsp light soy sauce
2 tbsp hoisin sauce
2 tbsp clear honey

2 garlic cloves, crushed
1 tsp sesame seeds

MARINADE:
1 dried red chilli
$^1/_2$-1 tsp chilli powder
$^1/_2$-1 ground ginger
finely grated rind of 1 lime

1 To make the marinade, crush the dried chilli in a pestle and mortar. Mix together the crushed dried chilli, chilli powder, ground ginger and lime rind in a small mixing bowl.

2 Thoroughly rub the spice mixture into the chicken wings with your fingertips. Set aside for at least 2 hours to allow the flavours to penetrate the chicken wings.

3 Heat the peanut oil in a preheated wok.

4 Add the chicken wings and fry, turning frequently, for 10–12 minutes, until golden and crisp. Drain off any excess oil.

5 Add the soy sauce, hoisin sauce, honey, garlic and sesame seeds to the wok, turning the chickens wings to coat them with the mixture.

6 Reduce the heat and cook for 20–25 minutes, turning the chicken wings frequently, until completely cooked through. Serve hot.

COOK'S TIP

*Make the dish in advance
and freeze the chicken wings.
Defrost thoroughly, cover with foil
and heat right through in a
moderate oven.*

Steamed Duck Buns

The dough used in this recipe may be wrapped around a wide variety of fillings, such as chicken, pork or prawns (shrimp), or sweet fillings as an alternative.

Serves 4

INGREDIENTS

DUMPLING DOUGH:
300 g/10^1/2 oz/2^2/3 cups plain (all-purpose) flour
15 g/^{1}/2 oz dried yeast
1 tsp caster (superfine) sugar
2 tbsp warm water
175 ml/6 fl oz/^{3}/4 cup warm milk

FILLING:
300 g/10^1/2 oz duck breast
1 tbsp light brown sugar
1 tbsp light soy sauce
2 tbsp clear honey
1 tbsp hoisin sauce
1 tbsp vegetable oil

1 leek, finely chopped
1 garlic clove, crushed
1-cm/^{1}/2-inch piece fresh root ginger (ginger root), grated

1 Place the duck breast in a large bowl. Mix together the sugar, soy sauce, honey and hoisin sauce. Pour the mixture over the duck and marinate for 20 minutes.

2 Remove the duck from the marinade and cook on a rack set over a roasting tin (pan) in a preheated oven, at 200°C/400°F/Gas Mark 6, for 35–40 minutes, or until cooked through. Leave to cool, remove the meat from the bones and cut into small cubes.

3 Heat the oil in a wok and fry the leek, garlic and ginger for 3 minutes. Mix with the duck meat.

4 Sift the flour into a large bowl. Mix the yeast, sugar and water in a separate bowl and leave in a warm place for 15 minutes. Pour the yeast mixture into the flour, together with the warm milk, mixing to form a firm dough.

5 Knead the dough on a floured surface for 5 minutes. Roll into a sausage shape, 2.5 cm/1 inch in diameter. Cut into 16 pieces, cover and let stand for 20–25 minutes.

6 Flatten the dough pieces into 10-cm/4-inch rounds. Place a spoonful of filling in the centre of each, draw up the sides to form a 'moneybag' shape and twist to seal.

7 Place the dumplings on a clean, damp tea towel (dish cloth) in the base of a steamer, cover and steam for 20 minutes.

Spinach Meatballs

These are somewhat of a surprise! Balls of pork mixture are coated in spinach and steamed before being served with a sesame and soy sauce dip.

Serves 4

INGREDIENTS

125 g/4^1/2 oz pork
1 small egg
1-cm/^{1}/2-inch piece fresh root ginger
  (ginger root), chopped
1 small onion, finely chopped
1 tbsp boiling water
25 g/1 oz canned bamboo shoots,
  drained, rinsed and chopped

2 slices smoked ham, chopped
2 tsp cornflour (cornstarch)
450 g/1 lb fresh spinach
2 tsp sesame seeds

SAUCE:
150 ml/^{1}/4 pint/^{2}/3 cup
  vegetable stock
^{1}/2 tsp cornflour (cornstarch)
1 tsp cold water
1 tsp light soy sauce
^{1}/2 tsp sesame oil
1 tbsp chopped chives

1 Mince (grind) the pork very finely in a food processor or meat mincer (grinder). Lightly beat the egg in a bowl and stir into the pork.

2 Put the ginger and onion in a separate bowl, add the boiling water and let stand for 5 minutes. Drain and add to the pork mixture with the bamboo shoots, ham and cornflour (cornstarch). Mix thoroughly and roll into 12 balls.

3 Wash the spinach and remove the stalks. Blanch in boiling water for 10 seconds and drain well, pressing out as much moisture as possible. Slice the spinach into very thin strips, then mix with the sesame seeds. Spread out the mixture in a shallow baking tin (pan). Roll the meatballs in the mixture to coat.

4 Place the meatballs on a heatproof plate in the base of

a steamer. Cover and steam for 8–10 minutes, until cooked through and tender.

5 Meanwhile, make the sauce. Put the stock in a saucepan and bring to the boil. Mix together the cornflour (cornstarch) and water to a smooth paste and stir it into the stock. Stir in the soy sauce, sesame oil and chives. Transfer the cooked meatballs to a warm plate and serve with the sauce.

Steamed Cabbage Rolls

These small cabbage parcels are quick and easy to prepare and cook. They are ideal for a speedy starter.

Serves 4

INGREDIENTS

8 cabbage leaves, trimmed
225 g/8 oz skinless, boneless chicken
175 g/6 oz peeled raw or cooked
   prawns (shrimp)

1 tsp cornflour (cornstarch)
1/2 tsp chilli powder
1 egg lightly beaten
1 tbsp vegetable oil

1 leek, sliced
1 garlic clove, thinly sliced
sliced fresh red chilli, to garnish

1 Bring a large saucepan of water to the boil. Blanch the cabbage leaves for 2 minutes. Drain, rinse under cold water and drain again. Pat dry with kitchen paper (paper towels) and spread out on a work surface (counter).

2 Put the chicken and prawns (shrimp) into a food processor and process until finely minced (ground). Alternatively, mince (grind) in a meat mincer (grinder). Transfer to a bowl and add the cornflour (cornstarch), chilli powder and egg, mixing together well.

3 Place 2 tablespoons of the chicken and prawn (shrimp) mixture towards one end of each cabbage leaf. Fold the sides of the cabbage leaf around the filling and roll up to form a firm parcel.

4 Arrange the parcels, seam-side down, in a single layer on a heatproof plate and cook in a steamer for 10 minutes, or until cooked through.

5 Meanwhile, heat the vegetable oil in a preheated wok. Add the leek and garlic and sauté for 1–2 minutes.

6 Transfer the cabbage parcels to warmed individual serving plates and garnish with red chilli slices. Serve with the leek and garlic sauté.

COOK'S TIP

Use Chinese cabbage or Savoy cabbage for this recipe, choosing leaves of a similar size for the parcels.

Chinese Omelette

This is a fairly filling omelette, as it contains chicken and prawns (shrimp).
It is cooked as a whole omelette and then sliced for serving.

Serves 4

INGREDIENTS

8 eggs
225 g/8 oz/2 cups cooked chicken,
   shredded

12 tiger prawns (jumbo shrimp),
   peeled and deveined
2 tbsp chopped chives

2 tsp light soy sauce
dash of chilli sauce
2 tbsp vegetable oil

1 Lightly beat the eggs in a large mixing bowl.

2 Add the shredded chicken and tiger prawns (jumbo shrimp) to the eggs, mixing well.

3 Stir in the chopped chives, soy sauce and chilli sauce, mixing well.

4 Heat the oil in a large frying pan (skillet) over a medium heat and add the egg mixture, tilting the pan to coat the base completely. Cook over a medium heat, gently stirring the omelette with a fork, until the surface is just set and the underside is a golden brown colour.

5 When the omelette is set, slide it out of the pan, with the aid of a palette knife (spatula).

6 Cut the omelette into squares or slices to serve.

VARIATION

You could add extra flavour to the omelette by stirring in 3 tbsp finely chopped fresh coriander (cilantro) or 1 tsp sesame seeds with the chives in step 3.

COOK'S TIP

Add peas or other vegetables to the omelette and serve as a main course for 2 people.

Main Courses

This comprehensive chapter covers many cooking methods and ingredients to give a very wide variety of main meals for all occasions, be it a simple supper, a dinner party or informal gathering. Fish, seafood, pork, lamb, beef, duck and chicken are all used to their full potential to delight the palette.

When choosing ingredients, try to purchase them as fresh as possible, particularly fish and seafood. You can vary the meat and fish used to suit your personal preference, as they are very adaptable recipes.

When entertaining, choose several different dishes to give as much variety of taste as possible, and prepare as much as you can in advance to enable you to spend more time with your guests than in the kitchen.

The portions in the recipes contained in this chapter are geared towards the traditional Chinese menu, and may be slightly smaller than a Western serving, so why not choose a selection and create your very own Chinese banquet!

Steamed Fish with Black Bean Sauce

The Chinese use a lot of whole fish in their cooking, and steaming is one of their preferred methods.
It helps maintain both the flavour and the texture.

Serves 4

INGREDIENTS

900 g/2 lb whole snapper, cleaned
    and scaled
3 garlic cloves, crushed
2 tbsp black bean sauce
1 tsp cornflour (cornstarch)

2 tsp sesame oil
2 tbsp light soy sauce
2 tsp caster (superfine) sugar
2 tbsp dry sherry
1 small leek, shredded

1 small red (bell) pepper, seeded and
    cut into thin strips
shredded leek and lemon wedges,
    to garnish
boiled rice or noodles, to serve

---

1 Rinse the fish inside and out with cold running water and pat dry with kitchen paper (paper towels). Make 2-3 diagonal slashes in the flesh on each side of the fish, using a sharp knife. Rub the garlic into the fish.

2 Thoroughly mix the black bean sauce, cornflour (cornstarch), sesame oil, light soy sauce, sugar and dry sherry together in a bowl. Place the fish in a shallow heatproof dish and pour the sauce mixture over the top.

3 Sprinkle the leek and (bell) pepper strips on top of the sauce. Place the dish in the top of a steamer, cover and steam for 10 minutes, or until the fish is cooked through. Transfer to a serving dish, garnish with shredded leek and lemon wedges and serve with boiled rice or noodles.

VARIATION

Whole sea bream or sea bass may be used in this recipe instead of snapper, if you prefer.

COOK'S TIP

Insert the point of a sharp knife into the fish to test if it is cooked. The fish is cooked through if the knife goes into the flesh easily.

Steamed Snapper with Fruit & Ginger Stuffing

Red mullet may be used instead of the whole snapper, although they are a little more difficult to stuff because of their size. Use one mullet per person.

Serves 4

INGREDIENTS

1.4 kg/3 lb whole snapper, cleaned and scaled
175 g/6 oz spinach
orange slices and shredded spring onion (scallion), to garnish

STUFFING:
60 g/2 oz/2 cups cooked long-grain rice
1 tsp grated fresh root ginger
2 spring onions (scallions), finely chopped

2 tsp light soy sauce
1 tsp sesame oil
$1/2$ tsp ground star anise
1 orange, segmented and chopped

1 Rinse the fish inside and out under cold running water and pat dry with kitchen paper (paper towels). Blanch the spinach for 40 seconds, rinse in cold water and drain well, pressing out as much moisture as possible. Arrange the spinach on a heatproof plate and place the fish on top.

2 To make the stuffing, mix together the cooked rice, grated ginger, spring onion (scallion), soy sauce, sesame oil, star anise and orange in a bowl.

3 Spoon the stuffing into the body cavity of the fish, pressing it in well with a spoon.

4 Cover the plate and cook in a steamer for 10 minutes, or until the fish is cooked through. Transfer the fish to a warmed serving dish, garnish with orange slices and shredded spring onion (scallion) and serve immediately.

COOK'S TIP

The name snapper covers a family of tropical and subtropical fish that vary in colour. They may be red, orange, pink, red, grey or blue-green. Some are striped or spotted and they range in size from about 15 cm/6 inches to 90 cm/3 ft.

Trout with Pineapple

Pineapple is widely used in Chinese cooking. The tartness of fresh pineapple complements fish particularly well.

Serves 4

INGREDIENTS

4 trout fillets, skinned
2 tbsp vegetable oil
2 garlic cloves, cut into slivers
4 slices fresh pineapple, peeled
 and diced

1 celery stick, sliced
1 tbsp light soy sauce
50 ml/2 fl oz/¼ cup fresh or
 unsweetened pineapple juice
150 ml/¼ pint/⅔ cup fish stock

1 tsp cornflour (cornstarch)
2 tsp water
shredded celery leaves and fresh red
 chilli strips, to garnish

1 Cut the trout fillets into strips. Heat 1 tablespoon of the vegetable oil in a preheated wok until almost smoking. Reduce the heat slightly, add the fish and sauté for 2 minutes. Remove from the wok and set aside.

2 Add the remaining oil to the wok, reduce the heat and add the garlic, pineapple and celery. Stir-fry for 1–2 minutes.

3 Add the soy sauce, pineapple juice and fish stock to the wok. Bring to the boil and cook, stirring, for 2–3 minutes, or until the sauce has reduced.

4 Blend the cornflour (cornstarch) with the water to form a paste and stir it into the wok. Bring the sauce to the boil and cook, stirring constantly, until the sauce thickens and clears.

5 Return the fish to the wok, and cook, stirring gently, until heated through. Transfer to a warmed serving dish and serve, garnished with shredded celery leaves and red chilli strips.

COOK'S TIP

Use canned pineapple instead of fresh pineapple if you wish, choosing slices in unsweetened, natural juice in preference to a syrup.

Szechuan White Fish

*Szechuan pepper is quite hot and should be used sparingly
to avoid making the dish unbearably spicy.*

Serves 4

INGREDIENTS

350 g/12 oz white fish fillets
1 small egg, beaten
3 tbsp plain (all-purpose) flour
4 tbsp dry white wine
3 tbsp light soy sauce
vegetable oil, for frying
1 garlic clove, cut into slivers

1-cm/^{1}/$_2$-inch piece fresh root
  ginger, finely chopped
1 onion, finely chopped
1 celery stick, chopped
1 fresh red chilli, chopped
3 spring onions (scallions), chopped
1 tsp rice wine vinegar

^{1}/$_2$ tsp ground Szechuan pepper
175 ml/6 fl oz/^{3}/$_4$ cup fish stock
1 tsp caster (superfine) sugar
1 tsp cornflour (cornstarch)
2 tsp water
chilli flowers and celery leaves,
  to garnish

1 Cut the fish into 4-cm/
1½-inch cubes.

2 In a mixing bowl, beat
together the egg, flour, wine
and 1 tablespoon of soy sauce to
make a batter.

3 Dip the cubes of fish into the
batter to coat well.

4 Heat the oil in a preheated
wok until it is almost
smoking. Reduce the heat slightly
and cook the fish, in batches, for
2–3 minutes, until golden brown.
Drain on kitchen paper (paper
towels), set aside and keep warm.

5 Pour all but 1 tablespoon of
oil from the wok and return
to the heat. Add the garlic, ginger,
onion, celery, chilli and spring
onions (scallions) and stir-fry for
1–2 minutes.

6 Stir in the remaining soy
sauce and the vinegar.

7 Add the Szechuan pepper, fish
stock and sugar to the wok.
Blend the cornflour (cornstarch)
with the water to form a smooth
paste and stir it into the stock.
Bring to the boil and cook,
stirring, for 1 minute, until the
sauce thickens and clears.

8 Return the fish to the wok
and cook for 1–2 minutes,
until hot. Transfer to a serving
dish, garnish with chilli flowers
and celery leaves and serve.

Crispy Fish

This is a very hot dish – not for the faint hearted! It may be made without the chilli flavourings, if preferred.

Serves 4

INGREDIENTS

450 g/1 lb white fish fillets

BATTER:
60 g/2 oz/½ cup plain
  (all-purpose) flour
1 egg, separated
1 tbsp peanut oil

4 tbsp milk
vegetable oil, for deep-frying

SAUCE:
1 fresh red chilli, chopped
2 garlic cloves, crushed
pinch of chilli powder

3 tbsp tomato purée (paste)
1 tbsp rice wine vinegar
2 tbsp dark soy sauce
2 tbsp Chinese rice wine
2 tbsp water
pinch of caster (superfine) sugar

1 Cut the fish into 2.5-cm/ 1-inch cubes and set aside. Sift the flour into a mixing bowl and make a well in the centre. Add the egg yolk and oil to the bowl and gradually stir in the milk, incorporating the flour to form a smooth batter. Leave to stand for 20 minutes.

2 Whisk the egg white until it forms peaks and fold it into the batter. Heat the oil in a preheated wok. Dip the fish into the batter and fry, in batches, for 8–10 minutes, until cooked through. Remove the fish from the wok with a slotted spoon, set aside and keep warm.

3 Pour off all but 1 tablespoon of oil from the wok and return to the heat. Add the chilli, garlic, chilli powder, tomato purée (paste), rice wine vinegar, soy sauce, Chinese rice wine, water and sugar and cook, stirring, for 3–4 minutes.

4 Return the fish to the wok and stir gently to coat it in the sauce. Cook for 2-3 minutes, until hot. Transfer the fish and sauce to a serving dish and serve immediately.

COOK'S TIP

Take care when pouring hot oil from the wok and ensure that you transfer it to a suitable bowl until cool.

Seafood Medley

Use any combination of fish and seafood in this delicious dish
of coated fish served in a wine sauce.

Serves 4

INGREDIENTS

2 tbsp dry white wine
1 egg white, lightly beaten
1/2 tsp Chinese five spice powder
1 tsp cornflour (cornstarch)
300 g/10 1/2 oz raw prawns (shrimp),
 peeled and deveined

125 g/4 1/2 oz prepared squid, cut
 into rings
125 g/4 1/2 oz white fish fillets, cut
 into strips
vegetable oil, for deep-frying

1 green (bell) pepper, seeded and cut
 into thin strips
1 carrot, cut into thin strips
4 baby corn cobs, halved lengthways

---

1 Mix together the wine, egg white, Chinese five spice powder and cornflour (cornstarch) in a large bowl. Add the prawns (shrimp), squid rings and fish fillets and stir to coat evenly. Remove the fish and seafood with a slotted spoon, reserving any leftover cornflour (cornstarch) mixture.

2 Heat the oil in a preheated wok and deep-fry the prawns (shrimp), squid and fish for 2–3 minutes. Remove the seafood

mixture from the wok with a slotted spoon and set aside.

3 Pour off all but 1 tablespoon of oil from the wok and return to the heat. Add the (bell) pepper, carrot and corn cobs and stir-fry for 4–5 minutes.

4 Return the seafood mixture to the wok and add any remaining cornflour mixture. Cook, stirring and tossing well to heat through. Transfer to a serving plate and serve immediately.

COOK'S TIP

Open up the squid rings
and using a sharp knife, score a
lattice pattern on the flesh to make
them look attractive.

Fried Prawns (Shrimp) with Cashews

Cashew nuts are delicious as part of a stir-fry with almost any other ingredient.
Use the unsalted variety in cooking.

Serves 4

INGREDIENTS

2 garlic cloves, crushed
1 tbsp cornflour (cornstarch)
pinch of caster (superfine) sugar
450 g/1 lb raw tiger prawns
   (jumbo shrimp)
4 tbsp vegetable oil

1 leek, sliced
125 g/4^1/$_2$ oz broccoli florets
1 orange (bell) pepper, seeded
   and diced
75 g/2^3/$_4$ oz/^{3}/$_4$ cup unsalted
   cashew nuts

SAUCE:
175 ml/6 fl oz/^{3}/$_4$ cup fish stock
1 tbsp cornflour (cornstarch)
dash of chilli sauce
2 tsp sesame oil
1 tbsp Chinese rice wine

1 Mix together the garlic, cornflour (cornstarch) and sugar in a bowl. Peel and devein the prawns (shrimp). Stir the prawns (shrimp) into the mixture to coat thoroughly.

2 Heat the oil in a preheated wok and add the prawn (shrimp) mixture. Stir-fry over a high heat for 20–30 seconds until the prawns (shrimp) turn pink. Remove the prawns (shrimp) from the wok with a slotted spoon and set aside.

3 Add the leek, broccoli and (bell) pepper to the wok and stir-fry for 2 minutes.

4 To make the sauce, mix together the fish stock, cornflour (cornstarch), chilli sauce to taste, the sesame oil and Chinese rice wine. Add the mixture to the wok, together with the cashew nuts. Return the prawns (shrimp) to the wok and cook for 1 minute to heat through. Transfer to a warm serving dish and serve immediately.

VARIATION

This recipe also works well with chicken, pork or beef strips instead of the prawns (shrimp). Use 225 g/8 oz meat instead of 450 g/1 lb prawns (shrimp).

(Small) Shrimp Fu Yong

*The classic ingredients of this popular dish are eggs, carrots and (small) shrimps.
Add extra ingredients such as peas or crabmeat, if desired.*

Serves 4

INGREDIENTS

2 tbsp vegetable oil
1 carrot, grated
5 eggs, beaten

225 g/8 oz raw (small) shrimp, peeled
1 tbsp light soy sauce
pinch of Chinese five spice powder

2 spring onions (scallions), chopped
2 tsp sesame seeds
1 tsp sesame oil

1 Heat the vegetable oil in a preheated wok.

2 Add the carrot and stir-fry for 1–2 minutes.

3 Push the carrot to one side of the wok and add the eggs. Cook, stirring gently, for 1–2 minutes.

4 Stir the (small) shrimp, soy sauce and five spice powder into the mixture in the wok. Stir-fry the mixture for 2–3 minutes, or until the (small) shrimps change colour and the mixture is almost dry.

5 Turn the (small) shrimp fu yong out on to a warm plate and sprinkle the spring onions (scallions), sesame seeds and sesame oil on top. Serve immediately.

VARIATION

For a more substantial dish, you could add 225 g/8 oz/1 cup cooked long-grain rice with the (small) shrimp in step 4. Taste and adjust the quantities of soy sauce, Chinese five spice powder and sesame oil if necessary. This is a useful way of using up leftover rice.

COOK'S TIP

If only cooked prawns (shrimp) are available, add them just before the end of cooking, but make sure they are fully incorporated into the fu yong. They require only heating through. Overcooking will make them chewy and tasteless.

Cantonese Prawns (Shrimp)

*This prawn (shrimp) dish is very simple and is ideal
for supper or lunch when time is short.*

Serves 4

INGREDIENTS

5 tbsp vegetable oil

4 garlic cloves, crushed

675 g/1¹/2 lb raw prawns (shrimp),
  shelled and deveined

5-cm/2-inch piece fresh root
  ginger, chopped

175 g/6 oz lean pork, diced

1 leek, sliced

3 eggs, beaten

shredded leek and red (bell) pepper
  matchsticks, to garnish

SAUCE:

2 tbsp dry sherry

2 tbsp light soy sauce

2 tsp caster (superfine) sugar

150 ml/¹/4 pint/²/3 cup fish stock

4¹/2 tsp cornflour (cornstarch)

3 tbsp water

1 Heat 2 tablespoons of the oil in a preheated wok. Add the garlic and stir-fry for 30 seconds. Add the prawns (shrimp) and stir-fry for 5 minutes, or until they change colour. Remove the prawns (shrimp) from the wok with a slotted spoon, set aside and keep warm.

2 Add the remaining oil to the wok and heat. Add the ginger, diced pork and leek and stir-fry over a medium heat for 4-5 minutes, or until the pork is lightly coloured and sealed.

3 Add the sherry, soy sauce, sugar and fish stock to the wok. Blend the cornflour with the water to form a smooth paste and stir it into the wok. Cook, stirring, until the sauce thickens and clears.

4 Return the prawns (shrimp) to the wok and add the beaten eggs. Cook for 5–6 minutes, gently stirring occasionally, until the eggs set. Transfer to a warm serving dish, garnish with shredded leek and (bell) pepper matchsticks and serve immediately.

COOK'S TIP

*If possible, use Chinese rice wine
instead of the sherry.*

Squid With Oyster Sauce

Squid is a delicious fish, which contrary to popular belief, is not rubbery. If prepared and cooked correctly, it is a quick cooking, attractive and tasty ingredient.

Serves 4

INGREDIENTS

450 g/1 lb squid
150 ml/¼ pint/⅔ cup vegetable oil
1-cm/½-inch piece fresh root
   ginger, grated

60 g/2 oz mangetout (snow peas)
5 tbsp hot fish stock
red (bell) pepper triangles, to garnish

SAUCE:
1 tbsp oyster sauce
1 tbsp light soy sauce
pinch of caster (superfine) sugar
1 garlic clove, crushed

1 To prepare the squid, cut down the centre of the body lengthways. Flatten the squid out, inside uppermost, and score a lattice design deep into the flesh, using a sharp knife.

2 To make the sauce, combine the oyster sauce, soy sauce, sugar and garlic in a small bowl. Stir to dissolve the sugar and set aside until required.

3 Heat the oil in a preheated wok until almost smoking. Lower the heat slightly, add the squid and stir-fry until they curl up. Remove with a slotted spoon and drain thoroughly on kitchen paper (paper towels).

4 Pour off all but 2 tablespoons of the oil and return the wok to the heat. Add the ginger and mangetout (snow peas) and stir-fry for 1 minute.

5 Return the squid to the wok and pour in the sauce and hot fish stock. Leave the mixture to simmer for 3 minutes, or until thickened.

6 Transfer to a warm serving dish, garnish with (bell) pepper triangles and serve immediately.

COOK'S TIP

Take care not to overcook the squid, otherwise it will be rubbery and unappetizing.

Scallops In Ginger Sauce

Scallops are both attractive and delicious and make this a special dish. Cooked with ginger and orange, this dish is perfect served with plain rice.

Serves 4

INGREDIENTS

2 tbsp vegetable oil
450 g/1 lb scallops, cleaned
 and halved
2.5-cm/1-inch piece fresh root
 ginger, finely chopped

3 garlic cloves, crushed
2 leeks, shredded
75 g/2^3/$_4$ oz/^{3}/$_4$ cup shelled peas
125 g/4^1/$_2$ oz canned bamboo
 shoots, drained and rinsed

2 tbsp light soy sauce
2 tbsp unsweetened orange juice
1 tsp caster (superfine) sugar
orange zest, to garnish

1 Heat the oil in a preheated wok. Add the scallops and stir-fry for 1–2 minutes. Remove the scallops from the wok with a slotted spoon and set aside.

2 Add the ginger and garlic to the wok and stir-fry for 30 seconds. Stir in the leeks and peas and cook, stirring, for a further 2 minutes.

3 Add the bamboo shoots and return the scallops to the wok. Stir gently to mix without breaking up the scallops.

4 Stir in the soy sauce, orange juice and sugar and cook for 1–2 minutes. Transfer to a serving dish, garnish with the orange zest and serve immediately.

COOK'S TIP

The edible parts of a scallop are the round white muscle and the orange and white coral or roe. The frilly skirt surrounding the muscle – the gills and mantle – may be used for making shellfish stock. All other parts should be discarded.

COOK'S TIP

Frozen scallops may be thawed and used in this recipe , adding them at the end of cooking to prevent them from breaking up. If you are buying scallops already shelled, check whether they are fresh or frozen. Fresh scallops are cream coloured and more translucent, while frozen scallops tend to be pure white.

Crab in Ginger Sauce

*In this recipe, the crabs are served in the shell for ease and visual effect
and coated in a glossy ginger sauce.*

Serves 4

INGREDIENTS

2 small cooked crabs
2 tbsp vegetable oil
9-cm/3-inch piece fresh root
   ginger, grated
2 garlic cloves, thinly sliced

1 green (bell) pepper, seeded and cut
   into thin strips
6 spring onions (scallions), cut into
   2.5-cm/1-inch lengths
2 tbsp dry sherry

$^{1}/_2$ tsp sesame oil
150 ml/$^{1}/_4$ pint/$^{2}/_3$ cup fish stock
1 tsp light brown sugar
2 tsp cornflour (cornstarch)
150 ml/$^{1}/_4$ pint/$^{2}/_3$ cup water

1 Rinse the crabs and gently loosen around the shell at the top. Using a sharp knife, cut away the grey tissue and discard. Rinse the crabs again.

2 Twist off the legs and claws from the crabs. Using a pair of crab claw crackers or a cleaver, gently crack the claws to break through the shell to expose the flesh. Remove and discard any loose pieces of shell.

3 Separate the body and discard the inedible lungs and sac.

Cut down the centre of each crab to separate the body into two pieces and then cut each of these in half again.

4 Heat the oil in a preheated wok. Add the ginger and garlic and stir-fry for 1 minute. Add the crab pieces and stir-fry for 1 minute.

5 Stir in the (bell) pepper, spring onions (scallions), sherry, sesame oil, stock and sugar. Bring to the boil, reduce the heat, cover and simmer for 3–4 minutes.

6 Blend the cornflour (cornstarch) with the remaining water and stir it into the wok. Bring to the boil, stirring, until the sauce is thickened and clear. Transfer to a warm serving dish and serve immediately.

COOK'S TIP

If preferred, remove the crabmeat from the shells prior to stir-frying and add to the wok with the (bell) pepper.

Chilli Chicken

*This is quite a hot dish, using fresh chillies. If you prefer
a milder dish, halve the number of chillies used.*

Serves 4

INGREDIENTS

350 g/12 oz skinless, boneless
  lean chicken
$^1/_2$ tsp salt
1 egg white, lightly beaten
2 tbsp cornflour (cornstarch)
4 tbsp vegetable oil

2 garlic cloves, crushed
1-cm/$^1/_2$-inch piece fresh root
  ginger, grated
1 red (bell) pepper, seeded and diced
1 green (bell) pepper, seeded
  and diced

2 fresh red chillies, chopped
2 tbsp light soy sauce
1 tbsp dry sherry or Chinese rice wine
1 tbsp wine vinegar

1 Cut the chicken into cubes
and place in a mixing bowl.
Add the salt, egg white, cornflour
(cornstarch) and 1 tablespoon of
the oil. Turn the chicken in the
mixture to coat thoroughly.

2 Heat the remaining oil in a
preheated wok. Add the garlic
and ginger and stir-fry for
30 seconds.

3 Add the chicken pieces to
the wok and stir-fry for
2–3 minutes, or until browned.

4 Stir in the (bell) peppers,
chillies, soy sauce, sherry or
Chinese rice wine and wine
vinegar and cook for a further
2–3 minutes, until the chicken is
cooked through. Transfer to a
warm serving dish and serve.

VARIATION

*This recipe works well if you use
350 g/12 oz lean steak, cut into thin
strips or 450 g/1 lb raw prawns
(shrimp) instead of the chicken.*

COOK'S TIP

*When preparing chillies,
wear rubber gloves to
prevent the juices from
burning and irritating your hands.
Be careful not to touch your face,
especially your lips or eyes until you
have washed your hands.*

Lemon Chicken

This is on everyone's list of favourite Chinese dishes, and it is so simple to make. Fried chicken is cooked in a tangy lemon sauce in minutes and is great served with stir-fried vegetables.

Serves 4

INGREDIENTS

vegetable oil, for deep-frying
650 g/1¹/₂ lb skinless, boneless
  chicken, cut into strips
lemon slices and shredded spring
  onion (scallion), to garnish

SAUCE:
1 tbsp cornflour (cornstarch)
6 tbsp cold water
3 tbsp fresh lemon juice

2 tbsp sweet sherry
¹/₂ tsp caster (superfine) sugar

1 Heat the oil in a preheated wok until almost smoking. Reduce the heat and stir-fry the chicken strips for 3–4 minutes, until cooked through. Remove the chicken with a slotted spoon, set aside and keep warm. Drain the oil from the wok.

2 To make the sauce, mix the cornflour with 2 tablespoons of the water to form a paste.

3 Pour the lemon juice and remaining water into the mixture in the wok. Add the

sherry and sugar and bring to the boil, stirring until the sugar has completely dissolved.

4 Stir in the cornflour mixture and return to the boil. Reduce the heat and simmer, stirring constantly, for 2-3 minutes, until the sauce is thickened and clear.

5 Transfer the chicken to a warm serving plate and pour the sauce over the top. Garnish with the lemon slices and shredded spring onion (scallion) and serve immediately.

COOK'S TIP

If you would prefer to use chicken portions rather than strips, cook them in the oil, covered, over a low heat for about 30 minutes, or until cooked through.

Chicken With Cashew Nuts & Vegetables

This is a popular dish in Chinese restaurants in the West, although nothing beats making it yourself.

Serves 4

INGREDIENTS

300 g/10 $^1/_2$ oz boneless, skinless chicken breasts
1 tbsp cornflour (cornstarch)
1 tsp sesame oil
1 tbsp hoisin sauce
1 tsp light soy sauce
3 garlic cloves, crushed

2 tbsp vegetable oil
75 g/2 $^3/_4$ oz/ $^3/_4$ cup unsalted cashew nuts
25 g/1 oz mangetout (snow peas)
1 celery stick, sliced
1 onion, cut into 8 pieces
60 g/2 oz beansprouts

1 red (bell) pepper, seeded and diced

SAUCE:
2 tsp cornflour (cornstarch)
2 tbsp hoisin sauce
200 ml/7 fl oz/ $^7/_8$ cup chicken stock

1 Trim any fat from the chicken breasts and cut the meat into thin strips. Place the chicken in a large mixing bowl. Sprinkle with the cornflour (cornstarch) and toss to coat the chicken strips in it, shaking off any excess. Mix together the sesame oil, hoisin sauce, soy sauce and 1 garlic clove. Pour this mixture over the chicken, turning to coat thoroughly. Leave to marinate for 20 minutes.

2 Heat half of the vegetable oil in a preheated wok. Add the cashew nuts and stir-fry for 1 minute, until browned. Add the mangetout (snow peas), celery, the remaining garlic, the onion, beansprouts and red (bell) pepper and cook, stirring occasionally, for 2–3 minutes. Remove the vegetables from the wok with a slotted spoon, set aside and keep warm.

3 Heat the remaining oil in the wok. Remove the chicken from the marinade and stir-fry for 3–4 minutes. Return the vegetables to the wok.

4 To make the sauce, mix the cornflour (cornstarch), hoisin sauce and chicken stock together and pour into the wok. Bring to the boil, stirring until thickened and clear. Serve immediately.

Chicken Chop Suey

Both well known and popular, chop suey dishes are easy to make and delicious. They are based on beansprouts and soy sauce with a meat or vegetable flavouring.

Serves 4

INGREDIENTS

4 tbsp light soy sauce
2 tsp light brown sugar
500 g/1¼ lb skinless, boneless
   chicken breasts
3 tbsp vegetable oil

2 onions, quartered
2 garlic cloves, crushed
350 g/12 oz beansprouts
3 tsp sesame oil

1 tbsp cornflour (cornstarch)
3 tbsp water
425 ml/¾ pint/2 cups chicken stock
shredded leek, to garnish

1 Mix the soy sauce and sugar together, stirring until the sugar has dissolved.

2 Trim any fat from the chicken and cut the meat into thin strips. Place the chicken strips in a shallow glass dish and spoon the soy mixture over them, turning to coat. Leave to marinate in the refrigerator for 20 minutes.

3 Heat the oil in a preheated wok. Add the chicken and stir-fry for 2–3 minutes, until golden brown.

4 Add the onions and garlic and cook for a further 2 minutes. Add the beansprouts, cook for a further 4–5 minutes, then add the sesame oil.

5 Blend the cornflour (cornstarch) with the water to form a smooth paste. Pour the stock into the wok, together with the cornflour paste and bring to the boil, stirring constantly until the sauce is thickened and clear. Transfer to a warm serving dish, garnish with shredded leek and serve immediately.

VARIATION

This recipe may be made with strips of lean steak, pork or with mixed vegetables. Change the type of stock accordingly.

Chicken with Yellow Bean Sauce

Ready-made yellow bean sauce is available from large supermarkets and Chinese food stores.
It is made from yellow soya beans and is quite salty in flavour.

Serves 4

INGREDIENTS

450 g/1 lb skinless, boneless
   chicken breasts
1 egg white, beaten
1 tbsp cornflour (cornstarch)
1 tbsp rice wine vinegar
1 tbsp light soy sauce

1 tsp caster (superfine) sugar
3 tbsp vegetable oil
1 garlic clove, crushed
1-cm/^{1}/$_2$-inch piece fresh root
   ginger, grated

1 green (bell) pepper, seeded
   and diced
2 large mushrooms, sliced
3 tbsp yellow bean sauce
yellow or green (bell) pepper strips,
   to garnish

1   Trim any fat from the chicken and cut the meat into 2.5-cm/1-inch cubes.

2   Mix the egg white and cornflour (cornstarch) in a shallow bowl. Add the chicken and turn in the mixture to coat. Set aside for 20 minutes.

3   Mix the vinegar, soy sauce and sugar in a bowl.

4   Remove the chicken from the egg white mixture.

5   Heat the oil in a preheated wok, add the chicken and stir-fry for 3–4 minutes, until golden brown. Remove the chicken from the wok with a slotted spoon, set aside and keep warm.

6   Add the garlic, ginger, (bell) pepper and mushrooms to the wok and stir-fry for 1–2 minutes.

7   Add the yellow bean sauce and cook for 1 minute. Stir in the vinegar mixture and return the chicken to the wok. Cook for 1–2

minutes and serve hot, garnished with (bell) pepper strips.

VARIATION

Black bean sauce would work equally well with this recipe. Although this would affect the appearance of the dish, as it is much darker in colour, the flavours would be compatible.

Crispy Chicken

In this recipe, the chicken is brushed with a syrup and deep-fried until golden.
It is a little time consuming, but well worth the effort.

Serves 4

INGREDIENTS

1.5 kg/3 lb 5 oz oven-ready chicken
2 tbsp clear honey
2 tsp Chinese five spice powder

2 tbsp rice wine vinegar
850 ml/1^1/$_2$ pints/3^3/$_4$ cups vegetable
  oil, for frying

chilli sauce, to serve

1 Rinse the chicken inside and out under cold running water and pat dry with kitchen paper (paper towels).

2 Bring a large saucepan of water to the boil and remove from the heat. Place the chicken in the water, cover and set aside for 20 minutes. Remove the chicken from the water and pat dry with kitchen paper (paper towels). Cool and leave to chill in the refrigerator overnight.

3 To make the glaze, mix the honey, Chinese five spice powder and rice wine vinegar.

4 Brush some of the glaze all over the chicken and return to the refrigerator for 20 minutes. Repeat this process until all of the glaze has been used up. Return the chicken to the refrigerator for at least 2 hours after the final coating.

5 Using a cleaver or heavy kitchen knife, open the chicken out by splitting it through the centre through the breast and then cut each half into 4 pieces.

6 Heat the oil for deep-frying in a wok until almost smoking. Reduce the heat and fry each piece of chicken for 5–7 minutes, until

golden and cooked through. Remove from the oil with a slotted spoon and drain on absorbent kitchen paper (paper towels).

7 Transfer to a serving dish and serve hot with a little chilli sauce.

COOK'S TIP

If it is easier, use chicken portions instead of a whole chicken. You could also use chicken legs for this recipe, if you prefer.

Spicy Peanut Chicken

This quick dish has many variations, but this version includes the classic combination of peanuts, chicken and chillies, blending together to give a wonderfully flavoured dish.

Serves 4

INGREDIENTS

300 g/10¹/₂ oz skinless, boneless
  chicken breast
2 tbsp peanut oil
125 g/4¹/₂ oz/1 cup shelled peanuts
1 fresh red chilli, sliced
1 green (bell) pepper, seeded and cut
  into strips

fried rice, to serve

SAUCE:
150 ml/¹/₄ pint/²/₃ cup chicken stock
1 tbsp Chinese rice wine or
  dry sherry
1 tbsp light soy sauce

1¹/₂ tsp light brown sugar
2 garlic cloves, crushed
1 tsp grated fresh root ginger
1 tsp rice wine vinegar
1 tsp sesame oil

1 Trim any fat from the chicken and cut the meat into 2.5-cm/ 1-inch cubes. Set aside.

2 Heat the peanut oil in a preheated wok. Add the peanuts and stir-fry for 1 minute. Remove the peanuts with a slotted spoon and set aside.

3 Add the chicken to the wok and cook for 1–2 minutes. Stir in the chilli and green (bell) pepper and cook for 1 minute.

Remove from the wok with a slotted spoon and set aside.

4 Put half of the peanuts in a food processor and process until almost smooth. Alternatively, place them in a plastic bag and crush them with a rolling pin.

5 To make the sauce, add the chicken stock, Chinese rice wine or dry sherry, soy sauce, sugar, garlic, ginger and rice wine vinegar to the wok.

6 Heat the sauce without boiling and stir in the peanuts, chicken, chilli and (bell) pepper.

7 Sprinkle the sesame oil into the wok, stir and cook for 1 minute. Serve hot with fried rice.

COOK'S TIP

If necessary, process the peanuts with a little of the stock in step 4 to form a softer paste.

Peking Duck

No Chinese cookery book would be complete without this famous recipe. Crispy skinned duck is served with pancakes and a tangy sauce for a really special meal.

Serves 4

INGREDIENTS

1.8 kg/4 lb duck
1.75 litres/3 pints/7^1/2 cups boiling
  water
4 tbsp clear honey
2 tsp dark soy sauce

2 tbsp sesame oil
125 ml/4 fl oz/^{1}/2 cup hoisin sauce
125 g/4^1/2 oz/^{2}/3 cup caster
  (superfine) sugar
125 ml/4 fl oz/^{1}/2 cup water

carrot strips, to garnish
Chinese pancakes, cucumber
  matchsticks and spring onions
  (scallions), to serve

1 Place the duck on a rack set over a roasting tin (pan) and pour 1.2 litres/2 pints/5 cups of the boiling water over it. Remove the duck and rack and discard the water. Pat dry with paper towels, replace the duck and the rack and set aside for several hours.

2 Mix together the honey, remaining boiling water and soy sauce. Brush the mixture over the skin and inside the duck. Reserve the remaining glaze. Set the duck aside for 1 hour, until the glaze has dried.

3 Coat the duck with another layer of glaze. Let dry and repeat until all of the glaze is used.

4 Heat the oil and add the hoisin sauce, sugar and water. Simmer for 2–3 minutes, until thickened. Cool and refrigerate.

5 Cook the duck in a preheated oven, at 190°C/375°F/Gas Mark 5, for 30 minutes. Turn the duck over and cook for 20 minutes. Turn the duck again and cook for 20–30 minutes, or until cooked through and the skin is crisp.

6 Remove the duck from the oven and set aside for 10 minutes. Meanwhile, heat the pancakes in a steamer for 5–7 minutes. Cut the skin and duck meat into strips, garnish with the carrot strips and serve with the pancakes, sauce, cucumber and spring onions (scallions).

COOK'S TIP

Keep the pancakes covered while working to prevent them from drying out.

Duck In Spicy Sauce

*Chinese five spice powder gives a lovely flavour to this sliced duck,
and the chilli adds a little subtle heat.*

Serves 4

INGREDIENTS

1 tbsp vegetable oil

1 tsp grated fresh root ginger

1 garlic clove, crushed

1 fresh red chilli, chopped

350 g/12 oz skinless, boneless duck
   meat, cut into strips

125 g/4$^1/_2$ oz cauliflower, cut
   into florets

60 g/2 oz mangetout (snow peas)

60 g/2 oz baby corn cobs,
   halved lengthways

300 ml/$^1/_2$ pint/1$^1/_4$ cups chicken
   stock

1 tsp Chinese five spice powder

2 tsp Chinese rice wine or dry sherry

1 tsp cornflour (cornstarch)

2 tsp water

1 tsp sesame oil

1 Heat the vegetable oil in a preheated wok. Lower the heat slightly and add the ginger, garlic, chilli and duck and stir-fry for 2-3 minutes. Remove from the wok with a slotted spoon and set aside.

2 Add the cauliflower florets, mangetout (snow peas) and baby corn cobs to the wok and stir-fry for 2-3 minutes. Pour off any excess oil from the wok and push the vegetables to one side.

3 Return the duck to the wok and pour in the stock. Sprinkle the Chinese five spice powder over the top, stir in the Chinese rice wine or sherry and cook over a low heat for about 15 minutes, until the duck is tender.

4 Blend the cornflour (cornstarch) with the water to form a paste and stir into the wok, together with the sesame oil. Bring to the boil, stirring until the sauce has thickened and cleared.

5 Transfer the duck and spicy sauce to a warm serving dish and serve immediately.

COOK'S TIP

Omit the chilli for a milder dish, or deseed the chilli before adding it to remove some of the heat.

Honey-glazed Duck

This honey and soy glaze gives a wonderful sheen and flavour to the duck skin.
This is such a simple recipe, yet the result is unutterably delicious.

Serves 4

INGREDIENTS

1 tsp dark soy sauce
2 tbsp clear honey
1 tsp garlic vinegar
2 garlic cloves, crushed

1 tsp ground star anise
2 tsp cornflour (cornstarch)
2 tsp water

2 large boneless duck breasts, about
225g/8 oz each
celery leaves, cucumber wedges and
snipped chives, to garnish

1 Mix together the soy sauce, clear honey, garlic vinegar, garlic and star anise. Blend the cornflour (cornstarch) with the water to form a smooth paste and stir it into the mixture.

2 Place the duck breasts in a shallow ovenproof dish. Brush with the soy marinade, turning to coat them completely. Cover and leave to marinate in the refrigerator for at least 2 hours, or overnight if possible.

3 Remove the duck from the marinade and cook in a preheated oven, at 220°C/425°F/ Gas Mark 7, for 20–25 minutes, basting frequently with the glaze.

4 Remove the duck from the oven and transfer to a preheated grill (broiler). Grill (broil) for about 3–4 minutes to caramelize the top.

5 Remove the duck from the grill (broiler) pan and cut into thin slices. Arrange the duck slices in a warm serving dish, garnish with celery leaves, cucumber wedges and snipped chives and serve immediately.

COOK'S TIP

If the duck begins to burn slightly while it is cooking in the oven, cover with foil. Check that the duck breasts are cooked through by inserting the point of a sharp knife into the thickest part of the flesh – the juices should run clear.

Duck With Mangoes

Use fresh mangoes in this recipe for a terrific flavour and colour.
If they are unavailable, use canned mangoes and rinse them before using.

Serves 4

INGREDIENTS

2 medium-size ripe mangoes
300 ml/$^1/_2$ pint/$1^1/_4$ cups
 chicken stock
2 garlic cloves, crushed
1 tsp grated fresh root ginger

3 tbsp vegetable oil
2 large skinless duck breasts, about
 225 g/8 oz each
1 tsp wine vinegar
1 tsp light soy sauce

1 leek, sliced
freshly chopped parsley, to garnish

1 Peel the mangoes and cut the flesh from each side of the stones (pits). Cut the flesh into strips.

2 Put half of the mango pieces and the stock in a food processor and process until smooth. Alternatively, press half of the mangoes through a fine sieve and mix with the stock.

3 Rub the garlic and ginger over the duck. Heat the oil in a preheated wok and cook the duck breasts, turning, until sealed.

Reserve the oil in the wok and remove the duck. Place the duck on a rack set over a roasting tin (pan) and cook in a preheated oven, at 220°C/425°F/Gas Mark 7, for 20 minutes, until cooked through.

4 Meanwhile, place the mango and stock mixture in a saucepan and add the vinegar and soy sauce. Bring to the boil and cook over a high heat, stirring, until reduced by half.

5 Heat the oil reserved in the wok and stir-fry the leek and

remaining mango for 1 minute. Remove from the wok, transfer to a serving dish and keep warm.

6 Slice the cooked duck breasts and arrange the slices on top of the leek and mango mixture. Pour the sauce over the duck slices, garnish and serve.

COOK'S TIP

Do not overcook the mango slices in the wok, or stir too vigorously, otherwise they will break up.

Stir-Fried Duck with Broccoli & (Bell) Peppers

This is a colourful dish using different coloured (bell) peppers and broccoli to make it both tasty and appealing to the eye.

Serves 4

INGREDIENTS

1 egg white
2 tbsp cornflour (cornstarch)
450 g/1 lb skinless, boneless
   duck meat
vegetable oil, for deep-frying

1 red (bell) pepper, seeded and diced
1 yellow (bell) pepper, seeded
   and diced
125 g/4¹/₂ oz small broccoli florets
1 garlic clove, crushed

2 tbsp light soy sauce
2 tsp Chinese rice wine or dry sherry
1 tsp light brown sugar
125 ml/4 fl oz/¹/₂ cup chicken stock
2 tsp sesame seeds

1 Beat the egg white and cornflour (cornstarch) together in a mixing bowl.

2 Cut the duck into 2.5-cm/ 1-inch cubes and stir into the egg white mixture. Leave to stand for 30 minutes.

3 Heat the oil for deep-frying in a preheated wok until almost smoking. Remove the duck from the egg white mixture, add to the wok and fry in the oil for

4–5 minutes, until crisp. Remove the duck from the oil with a slotted spoon and drain on kitchen paper (paper towels).

4 Add the (bell) peppers and broccoli to the wok and fry for 2–3 minutes. Remove with a slotted spoon and drain on kitchen paper (paper towels).

5 Pour all but 2 tablespoons of the oil from the wok and return to the heat. Add the garlic

and stir-fry for 30 seconds. Stir in the soy sauce, Chinese rice wine or sherry, sugar and stock and bring to the boil.

6 Stir in the duck and reserved vegetables and cook for 1–2 minutes.

7 Carefully spoon the duck and vegetables on to a warmed serving dish and sprinkle with the sesame seeds. Serve immediately.

Pork Fry with Vegetables

This is a very simple dish which lends itself to almost any combination of vegetables that you have to hand.

Serves 4

INGREDIENTS

350 g/12 oz lean pork
    fillet (tenderloin)
2 tbsp vegetable oil
2 garlic cloves, crushed
1-cm/^{1}/$_2$-inch piece fresh root
    ginger, cut into slivers

1 carrot, cut into thin strips
1 red (bell) pepper, seeded and diced
1 fennel bulb, sliced
25 g/1 oz water chestnuts, halved
75 g/2 ^{3}/$_4$ oz beansprouts
2 tbsp Chinese rice wine

300 ml/^{1}/$_2$ pint/1^1/$_4$ cups pork or
    chicken stock
pinch of dark brown sugar
1 tsp cornflour (cornstarch)
2 tsp water

1 Cut the pork into thin slices. Heat the oil in a preheated wok. Add the garlic, ginger and pork and stir-fry for 1–2 minutes, until the meat is sealed.

2 Add the carrot, (bell) pepper, fennel and water chestnuts to the wok and stir-fry for about 2-3 minutes.

3 Add the beansprouts and stir-fry for 1 minute. Remove the pork and vegetables from the wok and keep warm.

4 Add the Chinese rice wine, pork or chicken stock and sugar to the wok. Blend the cornflour (cornstarch) to a smooth paste with the water and stir it into the sauce. Bring to the boil, stirring constantly until thickened and clear.

5 Return the meat and vegetables to the wok and cook for 1–2 minutes, until heated through and coated with the sauce. Transfer to a warm serving dish and serve immediately.

COOK'S TIP

Use dry sherry instead of the Chinese rice wine if you have difficulty obtaining it.

Sweet & Sour Pork

This dish is a popular choice in Western diets, and must be one of the best known of Chinese recipes.

Serves 4

INGREDIENTS

150 ml/^{1}/$_4$ pint/^{2}/$_3$ cup vegetable oil, for deep-frying
225 g/8 oz pork fillet (tenderloin), cut into 1-cm/^{1}/$_2$-inch cubes
1 onion, sliced
1 green (bell) pepper, seeded and sliced
225 g/8 oz pineapple pieces
1 small carrot, cut into thin strips

25 g/1 oz canned bamboo shoots, drained, rinsed and halved
rice or noodles, to serve

BATTER:
125 g/4^1/$_2$ oz/1 cup plain (all-purpose) flour
1 tbsp cornflour (cornstarch)
1^1/$_2$ tsp baking powder
1 tbsp vegetable oil

SAUCE:
125 g/4^1/$_2$ oz/^{2}/$_3$ cup light brown sugar
2 tbsp cornflour (cornstarch)
125 ml/4 fl oz/^{1}/$_2$ cup white wine vinegar
2 garlic cloves, crushed
4 tbsp tomato purée (paste)
6 tbsp pineapple juice

1 To make the batter, sift the flour into a mixing bowl, together with the cornflour (cornstarch) and baking powder. Add the oil and stir in enough water to make a thick, smooth batter (about 175 ml/6 fl oz/ ^{3}/$_4$ cup).

2 Pour the vegetable oil into a wok and heat until almost smoking. Dip the cubes of pork into the batter, and cook in the hot oil, in batches, until the pork is cooked through. Remove the pork from the wok with a slotted spoon, set aside and keep warm.

3 Drain all but 1 tablespoon of oil from the wok and return it to the heat. Add the onion, (bell) pepper, pineapple pieces, carrot and bamboo shoots and stir-fry for 1–2 minutes. Remove from the wok with a slotted spoon and set aside.

4 Mix all of the sauce ingredients together and pour into the wok. Bring to the boil, stirring until thickened and clear. Cook for 1 minute, then return the pork and vegetables to the wok. Cook for a further 1–2 minutes, then transfer to a serving plate and serve with rice or noodles.

Pork with Plums

Plum sauce is often used in Chinese cooking with duck or rich, fattier meat to counteract the flavour.

Serves 4

INGREDIENTS

450 g/1 lb pork fillet
  (tenderloin)
1 tbsp cornflour (cornstarch)
2 tbsp light soy sauce
2 tbsp Chinese rice wine
4 tsp light brown sugar

pinch of ground cinnamon
5 tsp vegetable oil
2 garlic cloves, crushed
2 spring onions (scallions), chopped
4 tbsp plum sauce
1 tbsp hoisin sauce

150 ml/^{1}/4 pint/ ^{2}/3 cup water
dash of chilli sauce
fried plum quarters and spring
  onions (scallions), to garnish

1 Cut the pork fillet (tenderloin) into thin slices.

2 Mix the cornflour (cornstarch), soy sauce, rice wine, sugar and cinnamon together.

3 Place the pork in a shallow dish and pour the cornflour (cornstarch) mixture over it. Cover and leave to marinate for at least 30 minutes.

4 Remove the pork from the dish, reserving the marinade.

5 Heat the oil in a preheated wok. Add the pork and stir-fry for 3–4 minutes, until lightly coloured golden brown.

6 Stir in the garlic, spring onions (scallions), plum sauce, hoisin sauce, water and chilli sauce. Bring the sauce to the boil. Reduce the heat, cover and leave to simmer for 8–10 minutes, or until the pork is cooked through and tender.

7 Stir in the reserved marinade and cook, stirring, for about

5 minutes. Transfer to a warm serving dish and garnish with fried plum quarters and spring onions (scallions). Serve immediately.

VARIATION

Strips of boneless duck meat may be used instead of the pork, if you prefer.

Deep-fried Pork Fritters

Small pieces of pork are coated in a light batter and deep-fried in this recipe –
they are delicious dipped in a soy and honey sauce.

Serves 4

INGREDIENTS

450 g/1 lb pork fillet (tenderloin)
2 tbsp peanut oil
200 g/7 oz/1¾ cups plain (all-
  purpose) flour
2 tsp baking powder
1 egg, beaten

225 ml/8 fl oz/1 cup milk
pinch of chilli powder
vegetable oil, for deep-frying

SAUCE:
2 tbsp dark soy sauce

3 tbsp clear honey
1 tbsp wine vinegar
1 tbsp chopped chives
1 tbsp tomato purée (paste)
chives, to garnish

1 Cut the pork into 2.5-cm/ 1-inch cubes.

2 Heat the peanut oil in a preheated wok. Add the pork and stir-fry for 2-3 minutes, until sealed. Remove the pork with a slotted spoon and set aside until required.

3 Sift the flour into a mixing bowl and make a well in the centre. Gradually beat in the egg, milk and chilli powder to make a thick batter.

4 Heat the oil for deep-frying in a wok until almost smoking, then reduce the heat slightly.

5 Toss the pork pieces in the batter to coat thoroughly. Add the pork to the wok and deep-fry until golden brown and cooked through. Remove with a slotted spoon and drain well on absorbent kitchen paper (paper towels).

6 Meanwhile, mix together the soy sauce, honey, wine vinegar, chives and tomato purée

(paste) and spoon into a small serving bowl.

7 Transfer the pork fritters to serving dishes, garnish with chives and serve with the sauce.

COOK'S TIP

Be careful when heating the oil for deep-frying. It must be heated so that it is almost smoking, then the heat must be reduced immediately. Place the pork in the oil carefully.

Beef & Broccoli Stir-fry

This is a great combination of ingredients in terms of colour and flavour, and it is so simple and quick to prepare.

Serves 4

INGREDIENTS

225 g/8 oz lean steak, trimmed
2 garlic cloves, crushed
dash of chilli oil
1-cm/^{1}/2-inch piece fresh root
 ginger, grated

^{1}/2 tsp Chinese five spice powder
2 tbsp dark soy sauce
2 tbsp vegetable oil
150 g/5 oz broccoli florets
1 tbsp light soy sauce

150 ml/^{1}/4 pint/^{2}/3 cup beef stock
2 tsp cornflour (cornstarch)
4 tsp water
carrot strips, to garnish

1 Cut the steak into thin strips and place in a shallow glass dish. Mix together the garlic, chilli oil, grated ginger, Chinese five spice powder and soy sauce in a small bowl and pour over the beef, tossing to coat the strips evenly. Leave to marinate in the refrigerator.

2 Heat 1 tablespoon of the vegetable oil in a preheated wok. Add the broccoli and stir-fry over a medium heat for 4–5 minutes. Remove from the wok with a slotted spoon and set aside.

3 Heat the remaining oil in the wok. Add the steak together with the marinade, and stir-fry for 2-3 minutes, until the steak is browned and sealed.

4 Return the broccoli to the wok and stir in the soy sauce and stock.

5 Blend the cornflour (cornstarch) with the water to form a smooth paste and stir it into the wok. Bring to the boil, stirring, until thickened and clear. Cook for 1 minute.

6 Transfer the beef and broccoli stir-fry to a warm serving dish, arrange the carrot strips in a lattice on top and serve immediately.

COOK'S TIP

Leave the steak to marinate for several hours for a fuller flavour. Cover and leave to marinate in the refrigerator if preparing in advance.

Marinated Beef With Oyster Sauce

*This dish is quick to cook, but benefits from lengthy marinating,
as this tenderizes and flavours the meat.*

Serves 4

INGREDIENTS

225 g/8 oz lean steak, cut into
  2.5-cm/1-inch cubes
1 tbsp light soy sauce
1 tsp sesame oil
2 tsp Chinese rice wine or
  dry sherry
1 tsp caster (superfine)
  sugar
2 tsp hoisin sauce
1 garlic clove, crushed

$^1/_2$ tsp cornflour (cornstarch)
green (bell) pepper slices,
  to garnish
rice or noodles, to serve

SAUCE:
2 tbsp dark soy sauce
1 tsp caster (superfine) sugar
$^1/_2$ tsp cornflour (cornstarch)
3 tbsp oyster sauce

8 tbsp water
2 tbsp vegetable oil
3 garlic cloves, crushed
1-cm/$^1/_2$-inch piece fresh root
  ginger, grated
8 baby corn cobs, halved lengthways
$^1/_2$ green (bell) pepper, seeded and
  thinly sliced
25 g/1 oz bamboo shoots, drained
  and rinsed

---

1 Place the steak in a shallow dish. Mix together the soy sauce, sesame oil, Chinese rice wine or sherry, sugar, hoisin sauce, garlic and cornflour (cornstarch) and pour over the steak, turning it to coat completely. Cover and marinate for at least 1 hour.

2 Meanwhile, make the sauce. Mix the dark soy sauce with the sugar, cornflour (cornstarch), oyster sauce and water. Heat the oil in a preheated wok. Add the steak, together with the marinade, and stir-fry for 2–3 minutes, until sealed and lightly browned.

3 Add the garlic, ginger, baby corn cobs, (bell) pepper and bamboo shoots. Stir in the oyster sauce mixture and bring to the boil. Reduce the heat and cook for 2–3 minutes. Transfer to a warm serving dish, garnish with green (bell) pepper slices and serve immediately.

COOK'S TIP

For a fuller flavour, marinate the beef in the refrigerator overnight.

Spicy Beef

In this recipe beef is marinated in a five-spice and chilli marinade for a spicy flavour.

Serves 4

INGREDIENTS

225 g/8 oz fillet steak
2 garlic cloves, crushed
1 tsp powdered star anise
1 tbsp dark soy sauce
spring onion tassels, to garnish

SAUCE:
2 tbsp vegetable oil
1 bunch spring onions (scallions), halved lengthways
1 tbsp dark soy sauce

1 tbsp dry sherry
$1/4$ tsp chilli sauce
150 ml/$1/4$ pint/$2/3$ cup water
2 tsp cornflour (cornstarch)
4 tsp water

1 Cut the steak into thin strips and place in a shallow dish.

2 Mix together the garlic, star anise and dark soy sauce in a bowl and pour over the steak strips, turning them to coat thoroughly. Cover and leave to marinate in the refrigerator for at least 1 hour.

3 Heat the oil in a preheated wok. Reduce the heat, add the halved spring onions (scallions) and stir-fry for 1-2 minutes. Remove from the wok with a slotted spoon and set aside.

4 Add the beef to the wok, together with the marinade, and stir-fry for 3–4 minutes. Return the halved spring onions (scallions) to the wok and add the soy sauce, sherry, chilli sauce and two thirds of the water.

5 Blend the cornflour (cornstarch) to a paste with the remaining water and stir into the wok. Bring to the boil, stirring until the sauce thickens and clears.

6 Transfer to a warm serving dish, garnish with spring onion tassels and serve immediately.

COOK'S TIP

Omit the chilli sauce for a milder dish.

Beef & Beans

*The green of the beans complements the dark colour
of the beef, served in a rich sauce.*

Serves 4

INGREDIENTS

450 g/1 lb rump or fillet steak, cut
　　into 2.5-cm/1-inch pieces

MARINADE:
2 tsp cornflour (cornstarch)
2 tbsp dark soy sauce
2 tsp peanut oil

SAUCE:
2 tbsp vegetable oil
3 garlic cloves, crushed
1 small onion, cut into 8
225 g/8 oz thin green beans, halved
25 g/1 oz/$^1/_4$ cup unsalted cashews
25 g/1 oz canned bamboo shoots,
　　drained and rinsed

2 tsp dark soy sauce
2 tsp Chinese rice wine or dry sherry
125 ml/4 fl oz/$^1/_2$ cup beef stock
2 tsp cornflour (cornstarch)
4 tsp water
salt and pepper

1 To make the marinade,
mix together the cornflour
(cornstarch), soy sauce and
peanut oil.

2 Place the steak in a shallow
glass bowl. Pour the
marinade over the steak, turn to
coat thoroughly, cover and leave to
marinate in the refrigerator for at
least 30 minutes.

3 To make the sauce, heat the
oil in a preheated wok. Add
the garlic, onion, beans, cashews
and bamboo shoots and stir-fry for
2–3 minutes.

4 Remove the steak from the
marinade, drain, add to the
wok and stir-fry for 3–4 minutes.

5 Mix the soy sauce, Chinese
rice wine or sherry and beef
stock together. Blend the cornflour
(cornstarch) with the water and
add to the soy sauce mixture,
mixing to combine.

6 Stir the mixture into the wok
and bring the sauce to the
boil, stirring until thickened and
clear. Reduce the heat and leave to
simmer for 2–3 minutes. Season to
taste and serve immediately.

VARIATION

*This recipe would also be
delicious with the addition of sugar
snap peas instead of the beans,
if you prefer.*

Lamb Meatballs

These small meatballs are made with minced (ground) lamb and flavoured with chilli, garlic, parsley and Chinese curry powder.

Serves 4

INGREDIENTS

450 g/1 lb minced (ground) lamb
3 garlic cloves, crushed
2 spring onions (scallions), finely chopped
$^1/_2$ tsp chilli powder
1 tsp Chinese curry powder

1 tbsp chopped fresh parsley
25 g/1 oz/$^1/_2$ cup fresh white breadcrumbs
1 egg, beaten
3 tbsp vegetable oil
125 g/4$^1/_2$ oz Chinese cabbage, shredded

1 leek, sliced
1 tbsp cornflour (cornstarch)
2 tbsp water
300 ml/$^1/_2$ pint/1$^1/_4$ cups lamb stock
1 tbsp dark soy sauce
shredded leek, to garnish

1 Mix the lamb, garlic, spring onions, chilli powder, Chinese curry powder, parsley and breadcrumbs together in a bowl. Work the egg into the mixture, bringing it together to form a firm mixture. Roll into 16 small, even-sized balls.

2 Heat the oil in a preheated wok. Add the cabbage and leek and stir-fry for 1 minute. Remove from the wok with a slotted spoon and set aside.

3 Add the meatballs to the wok and fry in batches, turning gently, for 3-4 minutes, until golden brown all over.

4 Mix the cornflour (cornstarch) and water together to form a smooth paste and set aside. Pour the lamb stock and soy sauce into the wok and cook for 2–3 minutes. Stir in the cornflour (cornstarch) paste. Bring to the boil and cook, stirring constantly, until the sauce is thickened and clear.

5 Return the cabbage and leek to the wok and cook for 1 minute, until heated through. Arrange the cabbage and leek on a warm serving dish, top with the meatballs, garnish with shredded leek and serve immediately.

VARIATION

Use minced (ground) pork or beef instead of the lamb as an alternative.

Lamb with Mushroom Sauce

Use a lean cut of lamb, such as fillet, for this recipe
for both flavour and tenderness.

Serves 4

INGREDIENTS

350 g/12 oz lean boneless lamb, such
   as fillet or loin
2 tbsp vegetable oil
3 garlic cloves, crushed
1 leek, sliced
1 tsp cornflour (cornstarch)

4 tbsp light soy sauce
3 tbsp Chinese rice wine or
   dry sherry
3 tbsp water
1/2 tsp chilli sauce
175 g/6 oz large mushrooms, sliced

1/2 tsp sesame oil
fresh red chillies, to garnish

1 Using a sharp knife, cut the lamb into thin strips.

2 Heat the oil in a preheated wok. Add the lamb strips, garlic and leek and stir-fry for about 2-3 minutes.

3 Mix together the cornflour (cornstarch), soy sauce, Chinese rice wine or dry sherry, water and chilli sauce in a bowl and set aside.

4 Add the mushrooms to the wok and stir-fry for 1 minute.

5 Stir in the sauce and cook for 2–3 minutes, or until the lamb is cooked through and tender. Sprinkle the sesame oil over the top and transfer to a warm serving dish. Garnish with red chillies and serve immediately.

COOK'S TIP

Use rehydrated dried Chinese mushrooms obtainable from specialist shops or Chinese supermarkets for a really authentic flavour.

VARIATION

The lamb can be replaced with lean steak or pork fillet (tenderloin) in this classic recipe from Beijing. You could also use 2–3 spring onions (scallions), 1 shallot or 1 small onion instead of the leek, if you prefer.

Lamb with Garlic Sauce

This dish contains Szechuan pepper which is quite hot and may be replaced with black pepper, if preferred.

Serves 4

INGREDIENTS

450 g/1 lb lamb fillet or loin
2 tbsp dark soy sauce
2 tsp sesame oil
2 tbsp Chinese rice wine or dry sherry

$^{1}/_{2}$ tsp Szechuan pepper
4 tbsp vegetable oil
4 garlic cloves, crushed
60 g/2 oz water chestnuts, quartered

1 green (bell) pepper, seeded
  and sliced
1 tbsp wine vinegar
1 tbsp sesame oil
rice or noodles, to serve

1 Cut the lamb into 2.5-cm/ 1-inch pieces and place in a shallow dish.

2 Mix together 1 tablespoon of the soy sauce, the sesame oil, Chinese rice wine or sherry and Szechuan pepper. Pour the mixture over the lamb, turning to coat, and leave to marinate for 30 minutes.

3 Heat the vegetable oil in a preheated wok. Remove the lamb from the marinade and add to the wok, together with the garlic. Stir-fry for 2–3 minutes.

4 Add the water chestnuts and (bell) pepper to the wok and stir-fry for 1 minute.

5 Add the remaining soy sauce and the wine vinegar, mixing together well.

6 Add the sesame oil and cook, stirring constantly, for 1–2 minutes, or until the lamb is cooked through.

7 Transfer the lamb and garlic sauce to a warm serving dish and serve immediately with rice or noodles.

COOK'S TIP

Sesame oil is used as a flavouring, rather than for frying, as it burns readily, hence it is added at the end of cooking.

VARIATION

Chinese chives, also known as garlic chives, would make an appropriate garnish for this dish.

Hot Lamb

This really is quite a spicy dish, using 2 chillies in the rich sauce. Halve the number of chillies to reduce the heat or seed the chillies before using if desired.

Serves 4

INGREDIENTS

450 g/1 lb lean, boneless lamb
2 tbsp hoisin sauce
1 tbsp dark soy sauce
1 garlic clove, crushed
2 tsp grated fresh root ginger
2 tbsp vegetable oil
2 onions, sliced

1 fennel bulb, sliced
4 tbsp water

SAUCE:
1 large fresh red chilli, cut into
  thin strips

1 fresh green chilli, cut into
  thin strips
2 tbsp rice wine vinegar
2 tsp light brown sugar
2 tbsp peanut oil
1 tsp sesame oil

1 Cut the lamb into 2.5-cm/1-inch cubes and place in a shallow glass dish.

2 Mix together the hoisin sauce, soy sauce, garlic and ginger in a bowl and pour over the lamb, turning to coat well. Leave to marinate in the refrigerator for 20 minutes.

3 Heat the vegetable oil in a preheated wok. Add the lamb and stir-fry for 1–2 minutes.

4 Add the onions and fennel to the wok and cook for a further 2 minutes, or until they are just beginning to brown.

5 Stir in the water, cover and cook for 2–3 minutes.

6 To make the sauce, place the chillies, rice wine vinegar, sugar, peanut oil and sesame oil in a saucepan and cook over a low heat for 3-4 minutes, stirring to combine.

7 Transfer the lamb and onions to a warm serving dish, pour the sauce on top, toss lightly and serve immediately.

VARIATION

Use beef, pork or duck instead of the lamb and vary the vegetables, using leeks or celery instead of the onion and fennel.

Sesame Lamb Stir-Fry

This is a very simple, but delicious dish, in which lean pieces of lamb are cooked in sugar and soy sauce and sprinkled with sesame seeds, then served on a bed of leeks and carrot.

Serves 4

INGREDIENTS

450 g/1 lb boneless lean lamb
2 tbsp peanut oil
2 leeks, sliced
1 carrot, cut into matchsticks

2 garlic cloves, crushed
3 fl oz/85 ml/$\frac{1}{3}$ cup lamb or
  vegetable stock
2 tsp light brown sugar

1 tbsp dark soy sauce
4$\frac{1}{2}$ tsp sesame seeds

1 Cut the lamb into thin strips. Heat the peanut oil in a preheated wok. Add the lamb and stir-fry for 2–3 minutes. Remove the lamb from the wok with a slotted spoon and set aside.

2 Add the leek, carrot and garlic to the wok and stir-fry in the remaining oil for 1–2 minutes. Remove from the wok with a slotted spoon and set aside. Drain any remaining oil from the wok.

3 Place the lamb or vegetable stock, sugar and soy sauce in the wok and add the lamb. Cook,

stirring constantly to coat the lamb, for 2–3 minutes. Sprinkle the sesame seeds over the top, turning the lamb to coat.

4 Spoon the leek mixture on to a warm serving dish and top with the lamb. Serve immediately.

VARIATION

This recipe would be equally delicious made with strips of skinless chicken or turkey breast or with prawns (shrimp). The cooking times remain the same.

COOK'S TIP

Be careful not to burn the sugar in the wok when heating and coating the meat, otherwise the flavour of the dish will be spoiled.

Vegetables

Vegetables play a very important role in the Chinese diet and are used extensively in all meals. It is perfectly possible to enjoy a meal from a selection of the following recipes contained in this chapter, without including meat or fish.

The Chinese enjoy their vegetables crisp, so cooking times in this chapter reflect this factor in order to bring out the flavours and textures of the ingredients used, as well as preserving the vitamins and the brightness of the colours. There are main course dishes and a variety of side dishes, all of which bring out the full potential of vegetables.

When selecting vegetables for cooking, the Chinese attach great importance to the freshness of the ingredients used. Always buy crisp, firm vegetables, and cook them as soon as possible. Another point to remember is to wash the vegetables just before cutting, in order to avoid losing vitamins in water, and to cook them as soon as they have been cut so that the vitamin content is not lost through evaporation.

Spicy Aubergines (Eggplants)

Try to obtain the smaller Chinese aubergines (eggplants) for this dish, as they have a slightly sweeter taste, but the recipe is just as delicious with the larger variety.

Serves 4

INGREDIENTS

450 g/1 lb aubergines
  (eggplants), rinsed
2 tsp salt
3 tbsp vegetable oil
2 garlic cloves, crushed

2.5-cm/1-inch piece fresh root
  ginger, chopped
1 onion, halved and sliced
1 fresh red chilli, sliced
2 tbsp dark soy sauce
1 tbsp hoisin sauce

$^1/_2$ tsp chilli sauce
1 tbsp dark brown sugar
1 tbsp wine vinegar
1 tsp ground Szechuan pepper
300 ml/$^1/_2$ pint/1$^1/_4$ cups vegetable
  stock

1 Cut the aubergines (eggplants) into cubes if you are using the larger variety, or cut the smaller type in half. Place the aubergines (eggplants) in a colander and sprinkle with the salt. Let stand for 30 minutes. Rinse the aubergines (eggplants) under cold running water and pat dry with kitchen paper (paper towels).

2 Heat the oil in a preheated wok and add the garlic, ginger, onion and fresh chilli. Stir-fry for 30 seconds and add the aubergines (eggplants). Continue to cook for 1–2 minutes.

3 Add the soy sauce, hoisin sauce, chilli sauce, sugar, wine vinegar, Szechuan pepper and vegetable stock to the wok, reduce the heat and leave to simmer, uncovered, for 10 minutes, or until the aubergines (eggplants) are cooked. Increase the heat and boil to reduce the sauce until thickened enough to coat the aubergines (eggplants). Serve immediately.

COOK'S TIP

Sprinkling the aubergines (eggplants) with salt and letting them stand removes the bitter juices, which would otherwise taint the flavour of the dish.

Fried Tofu (Bean Curd) & Vegetables

Tofu (bean curd) may be obtained from both Chinese and Western supermarkets.
It is available in different forms, the cake form being used in this recipe.

Serves 4

INGREDIENTS

450 g/1 lb tofu (bean curd)
150 ml/$^1/_4$ pint/$^2/_3$ cup vegetable oil
1 leek, sliced
4 baby corn cobs, halved lengthways
60 g/2 oz mangetout (snow peas)
1 red (bell) pepper, seeded and diced

60 g/2 oz canned bamboo shoots,
  drained and rinsed
rice or noodles, to serve

SAUCE:
1 tbsp Chinese rice wine or
  dry sherry

4 tbsp oyster sauce
3 tsp light soy sauce
2 tsp caster (superfine) sugar
pinch of salt
50 ml/2 fl oz/$^1/_4$ cup vegetable stock
1 tsp cornflour (cornstarch)
2 tsp water

1 Rinse the tofu (bean curd) in cold water and pat dry with kitchen paper (paper towels). Cut the tofu (bean curd) into 2.5-cm/ 1-inch cubes.

2 Heat the oil in a preheated wok until almost smoking. Reduce the heat, add the tofu (bean curd) and stir-fry until golden brown. Remove from the wok with a slotted spoon and drain on absorbent kitchen paper (paper towels).

3 Pour all but 2 tablespoons of the oil from the wok and return to the heat. Add the leek, corn cobs, mangetout (snow peas), (bell) pepper and bamboo shoots and stir-fry for 2–3 minutes.

4 Add the Chinese rice wine or sherry, oyster sauce, soy sauce, sugar, salt and vegetable stock to the wok and bring to the boil. Blend the cornflour (cornstarch) with the water to form a smooth paste and stir it into the sauce.

Bring the sauce to the boil and cook, stirring constantly, until thickened and clear.

5 Stir the tofu (bean curd) into the mixture in the wok and cook for about 1 minute until hot. Serve with rice or noodles.

COOK'S TIP

Use marinated or smoked tofu for extra flavour.

Marinated Beansprouts & Vegetables

*This dish is served cold as a salad or appetizer and is very easy
to make. It is a form of cold chop suey.*

Serves 4

INGREDIENTS

450 g/1 lb beansprouts
2 fresh red chillies, seeded and finely
   chopped
1 red (bell) pepper, seeded and
   thinly sliced

1 green (bell) pepper, seeded and
   thinly sliced
60 g/2 oz water chestnuts, quartered
1 celery stick, sliced
3 tbsp rice wine vinegar

2 tbsp light soy sauce
2 tbsp chopped chives
1 garlic clove, crushed
pinch of Chinese curry powder

1 Place the beansprouts, chilli,
(bell) peppers, water
chestnuts and celery in a large
bowl and mix well.

2 Mix together the rice wine
vinegar, soy sauce, chives,
garlic and Chinese curry powder
in a bowl and pour over the
prepared vegetables. Toss to mix
thoroughly.

3 Cover the salad and leave to
chill for at least 3 hours.
Drain the vegetables thoroughly,
transfer to a serving dish and serve.

COOK'S TIP

*There are hundreds of varieties of
chillies and it is not always possible
to tell how hot they are going to be.
As a general rule, dark green
chillies are hotter than light green
and red chillies. Thin, pointed
chillies are usually hotter than fatter,
blunter chillies. However, there are
always exceptions and even chillies
from the same plant can vary
considerably in their degree of
spiciness. The heat of chillies is
measured in Scoville units.*

COOK'S TIP

*This dish is delicious with Chinese
roasted meats or served with the
marinade and noodles.*

Honey-fried Chinese Leaves (Cabbage)

*This vegetable is rather similar to lettuce in that the leaves
are delicate with a sweet flavour.*

Serves 4

INGREDIENTS

450 g/1 lb Chinese leaves (cabbage)
1 tbsp peanut oil
1-cm/$^{1}/_{2}$-inch piece fresh root
   ginger, grated
2 garlic cloves, crushed

1 fresh red chilli, sliced
1 tbsp Chinese rice wine or dry sherry
4$^{1}/_{2}$ tsp light soy sauce
1 tbsp clear honey

125 ml/4 fl oz/$^{1}/_{2}$ cup orange juice
1 tbsp sesame oil
2 tsp sesame seeds
orange zest, to garnish

1 Separate the Chinese leaves
(cabbage) and shred them
finely, using a sharp knife.

2 Heat the peanut oil in a
preheated wok. Add the
ginger, garlic and chilli to the wok
and stir-fry the mixture for about
30 seconds.

3 Add the Chinese leaves
(cabbage), Chinese rice wine
or sherry, soy sauce, honey and
orange juice to the wok. Reduce
the heat and leave to simmer for
5 minutes.

4 Add the sesame oil, sprinkle
the sesame seeds on top and
mix to combine. Transfer to a
warm serving dish, garnish
with the orange zest and serve
immediately.

COOK'S TIP

*Single-flower honey has a better,
more individual flavour than
blended honey. Acacia honey is
typically Chinese, but you could
also try clover, lemon blossom, lime
flower or orange blossom.*

VARIATION

*Use a cabbage, such as Savoy,
instead of Chinese leaves (cabbage)
if they are unavailable. The flavour
will be slightly different and the
colour darker, but it will still taste
just as delicious.*

Green Stir-fry

The basis of this recipe is pak choi, sometimes known as bok choy or Chinese greens.
If unavailable, use Swiss chard or Savoy cabbage instead.

Serves 4

INGREDIENTS

2 tbsp peanut oil
2 garlic cloves, crushed
1/2 tsp ground star anise
1 tsp salt

350 g/12 oz pak choi, shredded
225 g/8 oz baby spinach
25 g/1 oz mangetout (snow peas)
1 celery stick, sliced

1 green (bell) pepper, seeded
and sliced
50 ml/2 fl oz/1/4 cup vegetable stock
1 tsp sesame oil

1 Heat the peanut oil in a preheated wok.

2 Add the crushed garlic to the wok and stir-fry for about 30 seconds. Stir in the star anise, salt, pak choi, spinach, mangetout (snow peas), celery and green (bell) pepper and stir-fry for 3–4 minutes.

3 Add the stock, cover and cook for 3–4 minutes.

4 Remove the lid from the wok and stir in the sesame oil. Mix thoroughly.

5 Transfer the stir-fry to a warm serving dish and serve.

COOK'S TIP

Star anise is an important ingredient in Chinese cuisine. The attractive star-shaped pods are often used whole to add a decorative garnish to dishes. The flavour is similar to liquorice, but with spicy undertones and is quite strong. Together with cassia, cloves, fennel seeds and Szechuan pepper, dried star anise is used to make Chinese five spice powder.

COOK'S TIP

Serve this dish as part of a vegetarian meal or alternatively, with roast meats.

Creamy Green Vegetables

This dish is very quick to make. The Chinese leaves (cabbage) complement the leek perfectly.
A dash of cream is added to the sauce, but this may be omitted if preferred.

Serves 4

INGREDIENTS

450 g/1 lb Chinese leaves (cabbage), shredded

2 tbsp peanut oil

2 leeks, shredded

4 garlic cloves, crushed

300 ml/^{1}/$_2$ pint/1^1/$_4$ cups vegetable stock

1 tbsp light soy sauce

2 tsp cornflour (cornstarch)

4 tsp water

2 tbsp single (light) cream or natural (unsweetened) yogurt

1 tbsp chopped coriander (cilantro)

---

1 Blanch the Chinese leaves (cabbage) in boiling water for 30 seconds. Drain, plunge into cold water or rinse under cold running water, then drain thoroughly again.

2 Heat the oil in a preheated wok and add the Chinese leaves (cabbage), leeks and garlic. Stir-fry for 2–3 minutes.

3 Add the vegetable stock and soy sauce to the wok, reduce the heat to low, cover and simmer for 10 minutes, or until the vegetables are tender.

4 Remove the vegetables from the wok with a slotted spoon and set aside. Bring the stock to the boil and boil vigorously until reduced by about half.

5 Blend the cornflour (cornstarch) with the water and stir the mixture into the stock. Bring to the boil, and cook, stirring constantly, until thickened and clear.

6 Reduce the heat and stir in the vegetables and cream or yogurt. Cook over a low heat for 1 minute.

7 Transfer to a serving dish, sprinkle over the chopped coriander (cilantro) and serve.

COOK'S TIP

Do not boil the sauce once the cream or yogurt has been added, as it will separate.

Stir-Fried Cucumber with Chillies

*Warm cucumbers are absolutely delicious, especially when combined
with the heat of chilli and the flavour of ginger.*

Serves 4

INGREDIENTS

2 medium cucumbers
2 tsp salt
1 tbsp vegetable oil
2 garlic cloves, crushed

1-cm/^{1}/$_2$-inch fresh root
  ginger, grated
2 spring onions (scallions), chopped
2 fresh red chillies, chopped

1 tsp yellow bean sauce
1 tbsp clear honey
125 ml/4 fl oz/^{1}/$_2$ cup water
1 tsp sesame oil

1 Peel the cucumbers and cut in half lengthways. Scrape the seeds from the centre with a teaspoon and discard.

2 Cut the cucumber into strips and place on a plate. Sprinkle the salt over the cucumber strips and set aside for 20 minutes. Rinse well under cold running water and pat dry with absorbent kitchen paper (paper towels).

3 Heat the oil in a preheated wok until it is almost smoking. Lower the heat slightly and add the garlic, ginger, chilli and spring onions (scallions) and stir-fry for 30 seconds.

4 Add the cucumbers to the wok, together with the yellow bean sauce and honey. Stir-fry for a further 30 seconds.

5 Add the water and cook over a high heat until most of the water has evaporated.

6 Sprinkle the sesame oil over the cucumber and chilli stir-fry. Transfer to a warm serving dish and serve immediately.

COOK'S TIP

The cucumber is sprinkled with salt and left to stand in order to draw out the excess water, thus preventing a soggy meal!

Spicy Mushrooms

A mixture of mushrooms, common in Western cooking, have been used in this recipe for a richly flavoured dish. If Chinese dried mushrooms are available, add a small quantity for texture.

Serves 4

INGREDIENTS

2 tbsp peanut oil
2 garlic cloves, crushed
3 spring onions (scallions), chopped
300 g/10 oz button mushrooms
2 large open-cap mushrooms, sliced

125 g/4$^{1}/_{2}$ oz oyster mushrooms
1 tsp chilli sauce
1 tbsp dark soy sauce
1 tbsp hoisin sauce
1 tbsp wine vinegar

$^{1}/_{2}$ tsp ground Szechuan pepper
1 tbsp dark brown sugar
1 tsp sesame oil
chopped parsley, to garnish

1 Heat the oil in a preheated wok until almost smoking. Reduce the heat slightly, add the garlic and spring onions (scallions) and stir-fry for 30 seconds.

2 Add the mushrooms, chilli sauce, soy sauce, hoisin sauce, vinegar, pepper and sugar and stir-fry for 4–5 minutes, or until the mushrooms are cooked through.

3 Sprinkle the sesame oil on top. Transfer to a warm serving dish, garnish with parsley and serve immediately.

COOK'S TIP

Chinese mushrooms are used more for their unusual texture than for their flavour. Wood (tree) ears are widely used and are available dried from Chinese food stores. They should be rinsed, soaked in warm water for about 20 minutes and rinsed again before use. Straw mushrooms, so called because they grow on straw, are available, fresh or canned from Chinese food stores and some supermarkets. They have a slippery texture.

COOK'S TIP

This dish is ideal served with rich meat or fish dishes.

Garlic Spinach

This has to be one of the simplest recipes, yet it is so tasty. Spinach is quickly fried with garlic and lemon grass and tossed in a little soy sauce and sugar.

Serves 4

INGREDIENTS

900 g/2 lb fresh spinach
2 tbsp peanut oil
2 garlic cloves, crushed

1 tsp chopped lemon grass
pinch of salt

1 tbsp dark soy sauce
2 tsp brown sugar

1 Carefully remove the stems from the spinach. Rinse the spinach leaves and drain them thoroughly, patting them dry with absorbent kitchen paper (paper towels).

2 Heat the oil in a preheated wok until it is almost smoking.

3 Reduce the heat slightly, add the garlic and lemon grass and stir-fry for 30 seconds.

4 Add the spinach and salt to the wok and stir-fry for 2–3 minutes, or until the spinach has wilted.

5 Stir in the dark soy sauce and brown sugar and cook for a further 3–4 minutes. Transfer to a warm serving dish and serve immediately.

COOK'S TIP

Lemon grass is widely used in Asian cooking. It is available fresh, dried and canned or bottled. Dried lemon grass must be soaked for 2 hours before using. The stems are hard and are usually used whole and removed from the dish before serving. The roots can be crushed or finely chopped.

COOK'S TIP

Use baby spinach, if possible, as the leaves have a better flavour and look more appealing. If using baby spinach, the stems may be left intact.

Chinese Fried Vegetables

The Chinese are known for their colourful, crisp vegetables, quickly stir-fried. This recipe demonstrates how tasty they are, tossing them in a soy and hoisin sauce.

Serves 4

INGREDIENTS

2 tbsp peanut oil
350 g/12 oz broccoli florets
1 tbsp chopped fresh root ginger
2 onions, cut into 8
3 celery sticks, sliced
175 g/6 oz baby spinach

125 g/4^1/$_2$ oz mangetout
  (snow peas)
6 spring onions (scallions), quartered
2 garlic cloves, crushed
2 tbsp light soy sauce
2 tsp caster (superfine) sugar

2 tbsp dry sherry
1 tbsp hoisin sauce
150 ml/^{1}/$_4$ pint/^{2}/$_3$ cup vegetable
  stock

1 Heat the peanut oil in a preheated wok until it is almost smoking.

2 Add the broccoli florets, ginger, onions and celery and stir-fry for 1 minute.

3 Add the spinach, mangetout (snow peas), spring onions (scallions) and garlic and stir-fry for 3–4 minutes.

4 Mix together the soy sauce, sugar, sherry, hoisin sauce

and stock and pour into the wok, mixing well to coat the vegetables. Cover and cook over a medium heat for 2–3 minutes, or until the vegetables are cooked through, but still crisp. Transfer to a warm serving dish and serve immediately.

VARIATION

Any vegetables may be used in this recipe, depending on your preference and their seasonal availability.

COOK'S TIP

You could use this mixture to fill Chinese pancakes. They are available from Chinese food stores and can be reheated in a steamer in 2–3 minutes.

Vegetable Sesame Stir-fry

Sesame seeds add a delicious flavour to any recipe and are particularly good with vegetables in this soy and rice wine or sherry sauce.

Serves 4

INGREDIENTS

2 tbsp vegetable oil
3 garlic cloves, crushed
1 tbsp sesame seeds, plus extra
   to garnish
2 celery sticks, sliced
2 baby corn cobs, sliced

60 g/2 oz button mushrooms
1 leek, sliced
1 courgette (zucchini), sliced
1 small red (bell) pepper, sliced
1 fresh green chilli, sliced
60 g/2 oz Chinese leaves
   (cabbage), shredded

$^{1}/_{2}$ tsp Chinese curry powder
2 tbsp light soy sauce
1 tbsp Chinese rice wine or dry sherry
1 tsp sesame oil
1 tsp cornflour (cornstarch)
4 tbsp water

1 Heat the oil in a preheated wok until it is almost smoking. Lower the heat slightly, add the garlic and sesame seeds and stir-fry for 30 seconds.

2 Add the celery, baby corn, mushrooms, leek, courgette (zucchini), (bell) pepper, chilli and Chinese leaves (cabbage) and stir-fry for 4–5 minutes, until the vegetables are beginning to soften.

3 Mix together the Chinese curry powder, soy sauce, Chinese rice wine or sherry, sesame oil, cornflour (cornstarch) and water and stir the mixture into the wok. Bring to the boil and cook, stirring constantly, until the sauce thickens and clears. Cook for 1 minute, spoon into a warm serving dish, sprinkle sesame seeds on top and serve immediately.

VARIATION

You could substitute oyster sauce for the soy sauce, if you prefer.

COOK'S TIP

The ingredients are fried in vegetable oil in this recipe and not peanut oil as this would overpower the wonderful flavour of the sesame seeds. However, peanut oil could be used if desired.

Green Bean Stir-fry

*These beans are simply cooked in a spicy, hot sauce
for a tasty and very easy recipe.*

Serves 4

INGREDIENTS

450 g/1 lb thin green beans
2 fresh red chillies
2 tbsp peanut oil

$^1/_2$ tsp ground star anise
1 garlic clove crushed
2 tbsp light soy sauce

2 tsp clear honey
$^1/_2$ tsp sesame oil

1 Using a sharp knife, cut the green beans in half.

2 Slice the fresh chillies, seeding them first if you prefer a milder dish.

3 Heat the oil in a preheated wok until almost smoking.

4 Lower the heat slightly, add the green beans and stir-fry for 1 minute.

5 Add the sliced red chillies, star anise and garlic to the wok and stir-fry for a further 30 seconds.

6 Mix together the soy sauce, honey and sesame oil and stir into the wok. Cook for 2 minutes, tossing the beans in the sauce to coat. Transfer the beans to a warm serving dish and serve immediately.

VARIATION

This recipe is surprisingly delicious made with Brussels sprouts instead of green beans. Trim the sprouts, then shred them finely. Stir-fry the sprouts in hot oil for 2 minutes, then proceed with the recipe from step 4.

COOK'S TIP

This dish makes a great accompaniment to fish or lightly cooked meats with a mild flavour.

Vegetable Rolls

In this recipe a mixed vegetable stuffing is wrapped in Chinese leaves (cabbage) and steamed until tender. Serve with chilli or soy sauce for a really tasty meal.

Serves 4

INGREDIENTS

8 large Chinese leaves (Chinese cabbage leaves)

FILLING:
2 baby corn cobs, sliced
1 carrot, finely chopped

1 celery stick, chopped
4 spring onions (scallions), chopped
4 water chestnuts, chopped
2 tbsp unsalted cashews, chopped
1 garlic clove, chopped
1 tsp grated fresh root ginger

25 g/1 oz canned bamboo shoots, drained, rinsed and chopped
1 tsp sesame oil
2 tsp soy sauce

1 Place the Chinese leaves (cabbage leaves) in a large bowl and pour boiling water over them to soften them. Leave for 1 minute and drain thoroughly.

2 Mix together the baby corn cobs, carrot, celery, spring onions (scallions), water chestnuts, cashews, garlic, ginger and bamboo shoots in a bowl.

3 Mix together the sesame oil and soy sauce and add to the vegetables, mixing thoroughly.

4 Spread out the Chinese leaves (cabbage leaves) on a board and spoon an equal quantity of the filling mixture on to each leaf.

5 Roll the leaves up, folding in the sides, to make neat parcels. Secure the parcels with cocktail sticks (toothpicks).

6 Place the filled rolls in a small heatproof dish in a steamer, cover and cook for 15–20 minutes, until the parcels are cooked. Serve with a sauce of your choice.

COOK'S TIP

Make the parcels in advance, cover and store in the refrigerator until required, then steam according to the recipe.

Eight Jewel Vegetables

This recipe, as the title suggests, is a colourful mixture of eight vegetables, cooked in a black bean and soy sauce.

Serves 4

INGREDIENTS

2 tbsp peanut oil

6 spring onions (scallions), sliced

3 garlic cloves, crushed

1 green (bell) pepper, seeded and diced

1 red (bell) pepper, seeded and diced

1 fresh red chilli, sliced

2 tbsp chopped water chestnuts

1 courgette (zucchini), chopped

125 g/4^{1}/$_{2}$ oz oyster mushrooms

3 tbsp black bean sauce

2 tsp Chinese rice wine or dry sherry

4 tbsp dark soy sauce

1 tsp dark brown sugar

2 tbsp water

1 tsp sesame oil

1 Heat the peanut oil in a preheated wok until it is almost smoking.

2 Lower the heat slightly, add the spring onions (scallions) and garlic and stir-fry for about 30 seconds.

3 Add the (bell) peppers, chilli, water chestnuts and courgette (zucchini) to the wok and stir-fry for 2–3 minutes, or until the vegetables are just beginning to soften.

4 Add the mushrooms, black bean sauce, Chinese rice wine or sherry, soy sauce, sugar and water to the wok and stir-fry for a further 4 minutes.

5 Sprinkle with sesame oil and serve immediately.

VARIATION

Add 225 g/8 oz diced, marinated tofu (bean curd) to this recipe for a main meal for 4 people.

COOK'S TIP

Eight jewels or treasures form a traditional part of the Chinese New Year celebrations, which start in the last week of the old year. The Kitchen God, an important figure, is sent to give a report to heaven, returning on New Year's Eve in time for the feasting.

Spicy Vegetarian Fried Triangles

Marinated tofu (bean curd) is ideal in this recipe for added flavour,
although the spicy coating is very tasty with plain tofu (bean curd).

Serves 4

INGREDIENTS

1 tbsp sea salt
4$\frac{1}{2}$ tsp Chinese five spice powder
3 tbsp light brown sugar

2 garlic cloves, crushed
1 tsp grated fresh root ginger
2 x 225 g/8 oz cakes tofu (bean curd)

vegetable oil, for deep-frying
2 leeks, shredded and halved
shredded leek, to garnish

1 Mix the salt, Chinese five spice powder, sugar, garlic and ginger in a bowl and transfer to a plate.

2 Cut the tofu (bean curd) cakes in half diagonally to form two triangles. Cut each triangle in half and then in half again to form 16 triangles.

3 Roll the tofu (bean curd) triangles in the spice mixture, turning to coat thoroughly. Set aside for 1 hour.

4 Heat the oil for deep-frying in a wok until it is almost

smoking. Reduce the heat slightly, add the tofu (bean curd) triangles and fry for 5 minutes, until golden brown. Remove from the wok with a slotted spoon, set aside and keep warm.

5 Add the leeks to the wok and stir-fry for 1 minute. Remove from the wok with a slotted spoon and drain on absorbent kitchen paper (paper towels).

6 Arrange the leeks on a warm serving plate and place the fried tofu (bean curd) on top. Garnish with the fresh shredded leek and serve immediately.

COOK'S TIP

Fry the tofu (bean curd) in batches and keep each batch warm until all of the tofu (bean curd) has been fried and is ready to serve.

Bamboo Shoots, Ginger & (Bell) Peppers

This dish has a wonderfully strong ginger flavour which is integral to Chinese cooking. The mixed (bell) peppers give the otherwise insipid bamboo shoots a burst of colour.

Serves 4

INGREDIENTS

2 tbsp peanut oil

225 g/8 oz canned bamboo shoots, drained and rinsed

2.5-cm/1-inch piece fresh root ginger, finely chopped

1 small red (bell) pepper, seeded and thinly sliced

1 small green (bell) pepper, seeded and thinly sliced

1 small yellow (bell) pepper, seeded and thinly sliced

1 leek, sliced

125 ml/4 fl oz/^{1}/2 cup vegetable stock

1 tbsp light soy sauce

2 tsp light brown sugar

2 tsp Chinese rice wine or dry sherry

1 tsp cornflour (cornstarch)

2 tsp water

1 tsp sesame oil

1 Heat the peanut oil in a preheated wok.

2 Add the bamboo shoots, ginger, (bell) peppers and leek to the wok and stir-fry for 2–3 minutes.

3 Stir in the stock, soy sauce, sugar and Chinese rice wine or sherry and bring to the boil, stirring. Reduce the heat and simmer for 4–5 minutes, or until the vegetables begin to soften.

4 Blend the cornflour (cornstarch) with the water to form a smooth paste.

5 Stir the cornflour (cornstarch) paste into the wok. Bring to the boil and cook, stirring constantly, until the sauce thickens and clears.

6 Sprinkle the sesame oil over the vegetables and cook for 1 minute. Transfer to a warm serving dish and serve immediately.

COOK'S TIP

Add a chopped fresh red chilli or a few drops of chilli sauce for a spicier dish.

Bamboo Shoots with Spinach

In this recipe, spinach is fried with spices and then braised in a soy-flavoured sauce with bamboo shoots for a rich, delicious dish.

Serves 4

INGREDIENTS

3 tbsp peanut oil

225 g/8 oz spinach, chopped

175 g/6 oz canned bamboo shoots, drained and rinsed

1 garlic clove, crushed

2 fresh red chillies, sliced

pinch of ground cinnamon

300 ml/$\frac{1}{2}$ pint/$1\frac{1}{4}$ cups vegetable stock

pinch of sugar

pinch of salt

1 tbsp light soy sauce

---

1 Heat the peanut oil in a preheated wok.

2 Add the spinach and bamboo shoots to the wok and stir-fry for 1 minute.

3 Add the garlic, chilli and cinnamon to the mixture in the wok and stir-fry for a further 30 seconds.

4 Stir in the vegetable stock, sugar, salt and soy sauce, cover and cook over a medium heat for 5 minutes, or until the vegetables are cooked through and the sauce has reduced. Transfer the bamboo shoots and spinach to a warm serving dish and serve.

COOK'S TIP

Fresh bamboo shoots are rarely available in the West and, in any case, are extremely time-consuming to prepare. Canned bamboo shoots are quite satisfactory, as they are used to provide a crunchy texture, rather than for their flavour, which is fairly insipid.

COOK'S TIP

If there is too much liquid after 5 minutes cooking in step 4, blend a little cornflour (cornstarch) with double the quantity of cold water and stir into the sauce.

Sweet & Sour Tofu (Bean Curd) with Vegetables

Sweet-and-sour sauce was one of the first Chinese sauces introduced to Western diets, and remains one of the most popular. It is ideal with meat, fish or vegetables, as in this recipe.

Serves 4

INGREDIENTS

2 celery sticks
1 carrot
1 green (bell) pepper, seeded
75 g/3 oz mangetout (snow peas)
2 garlic cloves, crushed
2 tbsp vegetable oil

8 baby corn cobs
125 g/4¹/₂ oz beansprouts
450 g/1 lb tofu (bean curd), cubed
rice or noodles, to serve

SAUCE:
2 tbsp light brown sugar
2 tbsp wine vinegar
225 ml/8 fl oz/1 cup vegetable stock
1 tsp tomato purée (paste)
1 tbsp cornflour (cornstarch)

1 Thinly slice the celery, cut the carrot into thin strips, dice the (bell) pepper and cut the mangetout (snow peas) in half diagonally.

2 Heat the oil in a preheated wok until it is almost smoking. Reduce the heat slightly, add the garlic, celery, carrot, (bell) pepper, mangetout (snow peas) and corn cobs and stir-fry for 3–4 minutes.

3 Add the beansprouts and tofu (bean curd) to the wok and cook for 2 minutes, stirring well.

4 Combine the brown sugar, wine vinegar, vegetable stock, tomato purée (paste) and cornflour (cornstarch), stirring well to mix. Stir into the wok, bring to the boil and cook, stirring constantly, until the sauce thickens and clears. Continue to cook for 1 minute. Serve with rice or noodles.

COOK'S TIP

Be careful not to break up the tofu (bean curd) when stirring.

Gingered Broccoli

Ginger and broccoli are a perfect combination of flavours and make an exceptionally tasty side dish.

Serves 4

INGREDIENTS

2 tbsp peanut oil

1 garlic clove, crushed

5-cm/2-inch piece fresh root ginger, finely chopped

675 g/1¹/₂ lb broccoli florets

1 leek, sliced

75 g/2³/₄ oz water chestnuts, halved

¹/₂ tsp caster (superfine) sugar

125 ml/4 fl oz/¹/₂ cup vegetable stock

1 tsp dark soy sauce

1 tsp cornflour (cornstarch)

2 tsp water

1 Heat the oil in a preheated wok. Add the garlic and ginger and stir-fry for 30 seconds. Add the broccoli, leek and water chestnuts and stir-fry for a further 3–4 minutes.

2 Add the sugar, stock and soy sauce, reduce the heat and simmer for 4–5 minutes, or until the broccoli is almost cooked.

3 Blend the cornflour (cornstarch) with the water to form a smooth paste and stir it into the wok. Bring to the boil and cook, stirring constantly, for 1 minute. Transfer to a serving dish and serve immediately.

VARIATION

You could substitute spinach for the broccoli, if you prefer. Trim the woody ends and cut the remainder into 5-cm/2-inch lengths, keeping the stalks and leaves separate. Add the stalks with the leek in step 1 and add the leafy parts 2 minutes later. Reduce the cooking time in step 2 to 3–4 minutes.

COOK'S TIP

If you prefer a slightly milder ginger flavour, cut the ginger into larger strips, stir-fry as described and then remove from the wok and discard.

Chinese Potato Sticks

These potato sticks are a variation of the great Western favourite,
being flavoured with soy sauce and chilli.

Serves 4

INGREDIENTS

650 g/1¹/₂ lb medium-size potatoes
8 tbsp vegetable oil
1 fresh red chilli, halved
1 small onion, quartered

2 garlic cloves, halved
2 tbsp soy sauce
pinch of salt

1 tsp wine vinegar
1 tbsp coarse sea salt
pinch of chilli powder

1 Peel the potatoes and cut into thin slices along their length. Cut the slices into matchsticks.

2 Blanch the potato sticks in boiling water for 2 minutes, drain, rinse under cold water and drain well again. Pat thoroughly dry with absorbent kitchen paper (paper towels).

3 Heat the oil in a preheated wok until it is almost smoking. Add the chilli, onion and garlic and stir-fry for 30 seconds. Remove and discard the chilli, onion and garlic.

4 Add the potato sticks to the oil and fry for 3–4 minutes, or until golden.

5 Add the soy sauce, salt and vinegar to the wok, reduce the heat and fry for 1 minute, or until the potatoes are crisp.

6 Remove the potatoes with a slotted spoon and leave to drain on absorbent kitchen paper (paper towels).

7 Transfer the potato sticks to a serving dish, sprinkle with the sea salt and chilli powder and serve.

VARIATION

Sprinkle other flavourings over the cooked potato sticks, such as curry powder, or serve with a chilli dip.

Cucumber & Beansprout Salad

This is a very light dish and is ideal on its own
for a summer meal or as a starter.

Serves 4

INGREDIENTS

350 g/12 oz beansprouts
1 small cucumber
1 green (bell) pepper, seeded and cut
　into matchsticks
1 carrot, cut into matchsticks

2 tomatoes, finely chopped
1 celery stick, cut into matchsticks
1 garlic clove, crushed
dash of chilli sauce
2 tbsp light soy sauce

1 tsp wine vinegar
2 tsp sesame oil
16 fresh chives

1 Blanch the beansprouts in boiling water for 1 minute. Drain well and rinse under cold water. Drain thoroughly again.

2 Cut the cucumber in half lengthways. Scoop out the seeds with a teaspoon and discard. Cut the flesh into matchsticks and mix with the beansprouts, green (bell) pepper, carrot, tomatoes and celery.

3 Mix together the garlic, chilli sauce, soy sauce, vinegar and sesame oil. Pour the dressing over the vegetables, tossing well to coat. Spoon on to 4 individual serving plates. Garnish with fresh chives and serve.

VARIATION

You could substitute 350 g/12 oz cooked, cooled green beans or mangetout (snow peas) for the cucumber. Vary the beansprouts for a different flavour. Try aduki (adzuki) bean or alfalfa sprouts, as well as the better-known mung and soya bean sprouts.

COOK'S TIP

The vegetables may be prepared in advance, but do not assemble the dish until just before serving, otherwise the beansprouts will discolour.

Rice & Noodles

No Chinese cookbook would be complete without recipes for rice and noodle dishes. Many people believe that they should always serve rice with a savoury meal, and although it is often an excellent choice, there are many wonderful noodle dishes that can be served in its place.

Nevertheless, this chapter includes some delicious rice recipes which may be served as accompaniments or on their own. The Chinese use long-grain, short-grain or glutinous rice, and real experts would never use 'easy-cook' rice. Use whichever you are able to obtain for the recipes that follow and enjoy them! Fried rice is the most popular rice in Western restaurants, and so several variations have been included in this chapter.

A wide variety of noodles are available, made from wheat, buckwheat or rice flours. Noodles are used to their full potential in this chapter to bring you delicious accompaniments and main meal dishes.

Egg Fried Rice

This is a classic Chinese rice dish which has become very popular in the Western diet. Boiled rice is fried with peas, spring onions (scallions) and egg and flavoured with soy sauce.

Serves 4

INGREDIENTS

150 g/5^{1}/$_2$ oz/^{2}/$_3$ cup long-grain rice
3 eggs, beaten
2 tbsp vegetable oil
2 garlic cloves, crushed

4 spring onions (scallions), chopped
125 g/4^{1}/$_2$ oz/1 cup cooked peas
1 tbsp light soy sauce

pinch of salt
shredded spring onion (scallion), to
   garnish

1 Cook the rice in a saucepan of boiling water for 10-12 minutes, until almost cooked, but not soft. Drain well, rinse under cold water and drain thoroughly again.

2 Place the beaten eggs in a saucepan and cook over a gentle heat, stirring until softly scrambled.

3 Heat the oil in a preheated wok. Add the garlic, spring onions (scallions) and peas and sauté, stirring occasionally, for 1-2 minutes.

4 Stir the rice into the mixture in the pan, mixing to combine.

5 Add the eggs, soy sauce and salt to the wok and stir to mix the egg in thoroughly.

6 Transfer to serving dishes and serve garnished with the shredded spring onion (scallion).

VARIATION

You may choose to add prawns (shrimp), ham or chicken in step 3, if you wish.

COOK'S TIP

The rice is rinsed under cold water to wash out the starch and prevent it from sticking together.

Fried Rice with Pork

This dish is a meal in itself, containing pieces of pork,
fried with rice, peas, tomatoes and mushrooms.

Serves 4

INGREDIENTS

150 g/5^1/$_2$ oz/^{2}/$_3$ cup long-grain rice
3 tbsp peanut oil
1 large onion, cut into 8
225 g/8 oz pork tenderloin, thinly
  sliced

2 open-cap mushrooms, sliced
2 garlic cloves, crushed
1 tbsp light soy sauce
1 tsp light brown sugar

2 tomatoes, skinned, seeded and
  chopped
60 g/2 oz/^{1}/$_2$ cup cooked peas
2 eggs, beaten

1 Cook the rice in a saucepan of boiling water for about 15 minutes, until tender, but not soft. Drain well, rinse under cold running water and drain again thoroughly.

2 Heat the oil in a preheated wok. Add the sliced onion and pork and stir-fry for 3-4 minutes, until just beginning to colour.

3 Add the mushrooms and garlic to the wok and stir-fry for 1 minute.

4 Add the soy sauce and sugar to the mixture in the wok and stir-fry for a further 2 minutes.

5 Stir in the rice, tomatoes and peas, mixing well. Transfer the mixture to a warmed dish.

6 Stir the eggs into the wok and cook, stirring for 2-3 minutes, until beginning to set.

7 Return the rice mixture to the wok and mix well. Transfer to serving dishes and serve immediately.

COOK'S TIP

You can cook the rice in advance
and chill or freeze it until required.

Vegetable Fried Rice

*This dish can be served as part of a substantial meal for a number
of people or as a vegetarian meal in itself for four.*

Serves 4

INGREDIENTS

125 g/5 oz/^{2}/3 cup long-grain white
   rice
3 tbsp peanut oil
2 garlic cloves, crushed
^{1}/2 tsp Chinese five spice powder

60 g/2 oz/^{1}/3 cup green beans
1 green (bell) pepper, seeded and
   chopped
4 baby corn cobs, sliced
25 g/1 oz bamboo shoots, chopped

3 tomatoes, skinned, seeded and
   chopped
60 g/2 oz/^{1}/2 cup cooked peas
1 tsp sesame oil

1 Cook the rice in a saucepan
of boiling water for about
15 minutes. Drain well, rinse
under cold running water and
drain thoroughly again.

2 Heat the peanut oil in a
preheated wok.

3 Add the garlic and Chinese
five spice and stir-fry for
30 seconds.

4 Add the green beans, (bell)
pepper and corn cobs and
stir-fry for 2 minutes.

5 Stir the bamboo shoots,
tomatoes, peas and rice into
the mixture in the wok and stir-fry
for 1 further minute.

6 Sprinkle the vegetable fried
rice with sesame oil and
transfer to serving dishes. Serve
immediately.

VARIATION

*You could add cashew nuts , dry-
fried until lightly browned, in step
5 if you prefer.*

COOK'S TIP

*Use a selection of vegetables of your
choice in this recipe, cutting them
to a similar size in order to ensure
that they cook in the same
amount of time.*

Green-fried Rice

Spinach is used in this recipe to give the rice a wonderful green colouring.
Tossed with the carrot strips, it is a really appealing dish.

Serves 4

INGREDIENTS

150 g/5$\frac{1}{2}$ oz/$\frac{2}{3}$ cup long-grain rice
2 tbsp vegetable oil
2 garlic cloves, crushed

1 tsp grated fresh root ginger
1 carrot, cut into matchsticks
1 courgette (zucchini), diced

225 g/8 oz baby spinach
2 tsp light soy sauce
2 tsp light brown sugar

1 Cook the rice in a saucepan of boiling water for about 15 minutes. Drain the rice well, rinse under cold running water and then rinse the rice thoroughly again.

2 Heat the vegetable oil in a preheated wok.

3 Add the garlic and ginger to the wok and stir-fry for about 30 seconds.

4 Add the carrot and courgette (zucchini) to the mixture in the wok and stir-fry for about 2 minutes.

5 Add the baby spinach and stir-fry for 1 minute, until wilted.

6 Add the rice, soy sauce and sugar to the wok and mix together well.

7 Transfer the green-fried rice to serving dishes and serve immediately.

COOK'S TIP

Light soy sauce has more flavour than the sweeter, dark soy sauce, which gives the food a rich, reddish colour.

VARIATION

Chinese leaves may be used instead of the spinach, giving a lighter green colour to the dish.

Special Fried Rice

This dish is a popular choice in Chinese restaurants. Ham and prawns (shrimp)
are mixed with vegetables in a soy-flavoured rice.

Serves 4

INGREDIENTS

150 g/5^1/$_2$ oz/^{2}/$_3$ cup long-grain rice
2 tbsp vegetable oil
2 eggs, beaten
2 garlic cloves, crushed

1 tsp grated fresh root ginger
3 spring onions (scallions), sliced
75 g/3 oz/^{3}/$_4$ cup cooked peas
150 g/5^1/$_2$ oz/^{2}/$_3$ cup beansprouts

225 g/8 oz/1^1/$_3$ cups shredded ham
150 g/5^1/$_2$ oz peeled, cooked prawns
(shrimp)
2 tbsp light soy sauce

1 Cook the rice in a saucepan of boiling water for about 15 minutes. Drain well, rinse under cold water and drain thoroughly again.

2 Heat 1 tablespoon of the oil in a preheated wok and add the beaten eggs and a further 1 teaspoon of oil. Tilt the wok so that the egg covers the base to make a thin pancake. Cook until lightly browned on the underside, then flip the pancake over and cook on the other side for 1 minute. Remove from the wok and leave to cool.

3 Heat the remaining oil in the wok. Add the garlic and ginger and stir-fry for 30 seconds.

4 Add the spring onions (scallions), peas, beansprouts, ham and prawns (shrimp) to the wok and stir-fry for 2 minutes.

5 Stir in the soy sauce and rice and cook for a further 2 minutes. Transfer the rice to serving dishes.

6 Roll up the pancake, slice it very thinly and use to garnish the rice. Serve immediately.

COOK'S TIP

As this recipe contains meat and fish, it is ideal served with simpler vegetable dishes.

Chicken & Rice Casserole

This is a spicy casserole of rice, chicken, vegetables and chilli in a soy and ginger flavoured liquor. Although called a casserole, the dish only requires approximately 30 minutes cooking time.

Serves 4

INGREDIENTS

150 g/5¹/₂ oz/²/₃ cup long-grain rice
1 tbsp dry sherry
2 tbsp light soy sauce
2 tbsp dark soy sauce
2 tsp dark brown sugar
1 tsp salt

1 tsp sesame oil
900 g/2 lb skinless, boneless chicken
   meat, diced
850 ml/1¹/₂ pints/3³/₄ cups chicken
   stock
2 open-cap mushrooms, sliced

60 g/2 oz water chestnuts, halved
75 g/3 oz broccoli florets
1 yellow (bell) pepper, sliced
4 tsp grated fresh root ginger
whole chives, to garnish

1 Cook the rice in a saucepan of boiling water for about 15 minutes. Drain well, rinse under cold water and drain again thoroughly.

2 Place the sherry, soy sauce, sugar, salt and sesame oil in a large bowl and mix together until well combined.

3 Stir the chicken into the soy mixture, turning to coat well. Leave to marinate for about 30 minutes.

4 Bring the stock to the boil in a saucepan or preheated wok.

5 Add the chicken with the marinade, mushrooms, water chestnuts, broccoli, (bell) pepper and ginger.

6 Stir in the rice, reduce the heat, cover and cook for 25-30 minutes, until the chicken and vegetables are cooked through.

7 Transfer to serving plates, garnish with chives and serve.

VARIATION

This dish would work equally well with beef or pork. Chinese dried mushrooms may be used instead of the open-cap mushrooms, if rehydrated before adding to the dish.

Crab Fried Rice

Canned crabmeat is used in this recipe for convenience, but fresh white crabmeat could be used - quite deliciously - in its place.

Serves 4

INGREDIENTS

150 g/5^1/2 oz/^{2}/3 cup long-grain rice
2 tbsp peanut oil
125 g/4^1/2 oz canned white
    crabmeat, drained

1 leek, sliced
150 g/5^1/2 oz/^{2}/3 beansprouts
1 tbsp light soy sauce
2 tsp lime juice

2 eggs, beaten
1 tsp sesame oil
sliced lime, to garnish

1 Cook the rice in a saucepan of boiling salted water for 15 minutes. Drain well, rinse under cold running water and drain again thoroughly.

2 Heat the peanut oil in a preheated wok.

3 Add the crabmeat, leek and beansprouts to the wok and stir-fry for 2-3 minutes. Remove the mixture with a slotted spoon and set aside until required.

4 Add the eggs to the wok and cook, stirring occasionally, for 2-3 minutes, until they begin to set.

5 Stir the rice and the crabmeat, leek and beansprout mixture into the eggs in the wok.

6 Add the soy sauce and lime juice to the mixture in the wok. Cook for 1 minute, stirring to combine, and sprinkle with the sesame oil.

7 Transfer the crab fried rice to a serving dish, garnish with the sliced lime and serve immediately.

VARIATION

Cooked lobster may be used instead of the crab for a really special dish.

Fried Vegetable Noodles

*In this recipe, noodles are first boiled and then deep-fried for
a crisply textured dish, and tossed with fried vegetables.*

Serves 4

INGREDIENTS

350 g/12 oz/3 cups dried egg noodles
2 tbsp peanut oil
2 garlic cloves, crushed
1/2 tsp ground star anise
1 carrot, cut into matchsticks

1 green (bell) pepper, cut into
  matchsticks
1 onion, quartered and sliced
125 g/4 1/2 oz broccoli florets
75 g/3 oz bamboo shoots
1 celery stick, sliced

1 tbsp light soy sauce
150 ml/1/4 pint/2/3 cup vegetable
  stock
1 tsp cornflour (cornstarch)
2 tsp water
oil, for deep-frying

1 Cook the noodles in boiling water for 1-2 minutes. Drain well and rinse under cold running water. Leave to drain in a colander.

2 Heat the oil in a preheated wok until smoking. Reduce the heat, add the garlic and star anise and stir-fry for 30 seconds. Add the remaining vegetables and stir-fry for 1-2 minutes.

3 Add the soy sauce and stock to the wok and cook over a low heat for 5 minutes.

4 Heat the oil for deep-frying to 180°C/350°F, or until a cube of bread browns in 30 seconds.

5 Form the drained noodles into rounds and deep-fry them in batches until crisp, turning once. Leave to drain on kitchen paper (paper towels).

6 Blend the cornflour (cornstarch) with the water to form a paste and stir into the wok. Bring to the boil, stirring until the sauce is thickened and clear.

7 Arrange the noodles on a warm serving plate, spoon the vegetables on top and serve immediately.

COOK'S TIP

Make sure that the noodles are very dry before adding them to the hot oil, otherwise the oil will spit.

Curried Prawn (Shrimp) Noodles

These noodles have a fairly strong flavour and are almost a meal in themselves. If served as an accompaniment, they are ideal with plain vegetable or fish dishes.

Serves 4

INGREDIENTS

225 g/8 oz rice noodles
4 tbsp vegetable oil
1 onion, sliced
2 ham slices, shredded
2 tbsp Chinese curry powder

150 ml/$^1/_4$ pint/$^2/_3$ cups fish stock
225 g/8 oz peeled, raw prawns (shrimp)
2 garlic cloves, crushed
6 spring onions (scallions), chopped

1 tbsp light soy sauce
2 tbsp hoisin sauce
1 tbsp dry sherry
2 tsp lime juice
fresh chives, to garnish

1 Cook the rice noodles in a saucepan of boiling water for 3-4 minutes. Drain well, rinse under cold water and drain thoroughly again. Set aside until required.

2 Heat 2 tablespoons of the oil in a preheated wok.

3 Add the onion and ham and stir-fry for 1 minute.

4 Add the curry powder to the mixture in the wok and stir-fry for a further 30 seconds.

5 Stir the noodles and stock into the wok and cook for 2-3 minutes. Remove the noodles from the wok and keep warm.

6 Heat the remaining oil in the wok. Add the prawns (shrimp), garlic and spring onions (scallions) and stir-fry for about 1 minute.

7 Add the soy sauce, hoisin sauce, sherry and lime juice and stir to combine. Pour the mixture over the noodles, toss to mix and garnish with fresh chives.

VARIATION

You can use cooked prawns (shrimp) if you prefer, but toss them into the mixture at the last minute – long enough for them to heat right through. Overcooking will result in tough, inedible prawns (shrimp).

Cellophane Noodles with Yellow Bean Sauce

Cellophane or thread noodles are excellent re-heated, unlike other noodles which must be served as soon as they are ready.

Serves 4

INGREDIENTS

175 g/6 oz cellophane noodles
1 tbsp peanut oil
1 leek, sliced
2 garlic cloves, crushed

450 g/1 lb minced (ground) chicken
450 ml/$^3/_4$ pint/1 cup chicken stock
1 tsp chilli sauce
2 tbsp yellow bean sauce

4 tbsp light soy sauce
1 tsp sesame oil
chopped chives, to garnish

1 Soak the noodles in boiling water for 15 minutes. Drain the noodles thoroughly and cut them into short lengths with a pair of kitchen scissors.

2 Heat the oil in a preheated wok. Add the leek and garlic and stir-fry for 30 seconds.

3 Add the chicken to the mixture in the wok and stir-fry for 4-5 minutes, until the chicken is completely cooked through.

4 Add the chicken stock, chilli sauce, yellow bean sauce and soy sauce to the wok and cook for 3-4 minutes.

5 Add the drained noodles and sesame oil to the wok and cook, tossing to mix well, for 4-5 minutes.

6 Spoon the cellophane noodles and yellow bean sauce into warm serving bowls, sprinkle with chopped chives and serve immediately.

COOK'S TIP

Cellophane noodles are available from many supermarkets and all Chinese supermarkets.

Noodles with Prawns (Shrimp)

*This is a simple dish using egg noodles and large prawns (shrimp),
which give the dish a wonderful flavour, texture and colour.*

Serves 4

INGREDIENTS

225 g/8 oz thin egg noodles
2 tbsp peanut oil
1 garlic clove, crushed
1/2 tsp ground star anise

1 bunch spring onions (scallions), cut
  into 5-cm/2-inch pieces
24 raw tiger prawns (jumbo shrimp),
  peeled with tails intact

2 tbsp light soy sauce
2 tsp lime juice
lime wedges, to garnish

1 Blanch the noodles in a saucepan of boiling water for about 2 minutes. Drain well, rinse under cold water and drain thoroughly again.

2 Heat the oil in a preheated wok until almost smoking.

3 Add the garlic and star anise to the wok and stir-fry for 30 seconds.

4 Add the spring onions (scallions) and prawns (shrimp) to the wok and stir-fry for 2-3 minutes.

5 Stir in the soy sauce, lime juice and noodles and mix well. Cook for 1 minute, then spoon into a warm serving dish. Transfer to serving bowls, garnish with lime wedges and serve immediately.

COOK'S TIP

Chinese egg noodles are made from wheat or rice flour, water and egg. Noodles are a symbol of longevity, and so are always served at birthday celebrations – it is regarded as bad luck to cut them.

VARIATION

This dish is just as tasty with smaller cooked prawns (shrimp), but it is not quite so visually appealing.

Beef Chow Mein

Chow Mein must be the best-known and most popular noodle dish on any Chinese menu. Beef is used in this recipe, but you could use chicken, pork or vegetables instead.

Serves 4

INGREDIENTS

450 g/1 lb egg noodles
4 tbsp peanut oil
450 g/1 lb lean beef steak, cut into
 thin strips
2 garlic cloves, crushed

1 tsp grated fresh root ginger
1 green (bell) pepper, thinly sliced
1 carrot, thinly sliced
2 celery sticks, sliced
8 spring onions (scallions)

1 tsp dark brown sugar
1 tbsp dry sherry
2 tbsp dark soy sauce
few drops of chilli sauce

1 Cook the noodles in a saucepan of boiling salted water for 4-5 minutes. Drain well, rinse under cold running water and drain thoroughly again.

2 Toss the noodles in 1 tablespoon of the oil.

3 Heat the remaining oil in a preheated wok. Add the beef and stir-fry for 3-4 minutes, stirring constantly.

4 Add the garlic and ginger and stir-fry for 30 seconds.

5 Add the (bell) pepper, carrot, celery and spring onions (scallions) and stir-fry for about 2 minutes.

6 Add the sugar, sherry, soy sauce and chilli sauce and cook, stirring, for 1 minute.

7 Stir in the noodles, mixing well, and cook until completely warmed through.

8 Transfer the noodles to warm serving bowls and serve immediately.

VARIATION

A variety of different vegetables may be used in this recipe for colour and flavour – try broccoli, red (bell) peppers, green beans or baby sweetcorn cobs.

Cellophane Noodles with Prawns (Shrimp)

In this recipe, tiger prawns (jumbo shrimp) are cooked with orange juice, (bell) peppers, soy sauce and vinegar and served on a bed of cellophane noodles for a truly wonderful dish.

Serves 4

INGREDIENTS

175 g/6 oz cellophane noodles
1 tbsp vegetable oil
1 garlic clove, crushed
2 tsp grated fresh root ginger
24 raw tiger prawns (jumbo shrimp), peeled and deveined

1 red (bell) pepper, seeded and thinly sliced
1 green (bell) pepper, seeded and thinly sliced
1 onion, chopped
2 tbsp light soy sauce
juice of 1 orange

2 tsp wine vinegar
pinch of brown sugar
150 ml/^{1}/4 pint/^{2}/3 cup fish stock
1 tbsp cornflour (cornstarch)
2 tsp water
orange slices, to garnish

1 Cook the noodles in a saucepan of boiling water for 1 minute. Drain well, rinse under cold water and then drain thoroughly again.

2 Heat the oil in a preheated wok. Add the garlic and ginger and stir-fry for 30 seconds.

3 Add the prawns (shrimp) and stir-fry for 2 minutes. Remove the prawns (shrimp) with a slotted spoon and keep warm.

4 Add the (bell) peppers and onion to the wok and stir-fry for 2 minutes. Stir in the soy sauce, orange juice, vinegar, sugar and stock.

5 Return the prawns (shrimp) to the wok and cook for 8-10 minutes, until cooked through.

6 Blend the cornflour (cornstarch) with the water and add to the wok. Bring to the boil, add the noodles and cook for 1-2 minutes. Garnish and serve.

VARIATION

Lime or lemon juice and slices may be used instead of the orange. Use 3-5^1/2 tsp of these juices.

Desserts

Desserts are almost unheard of in ordinary Chinese households and the following recipes are adaptations of Imperial recipes or use Chinese cooking methods and ingredients to produce delicious desserts which would round off any meal perfectly.

The Chinese do not usually have desserts to finish off a meal, except at banquets and special occasions. Sweet dishes are usually served in between main meals as snacks, but fresh fruit is considered to be very refreshing at the end of a big meal.

Rice is cooked with fruits, lychees are spiced with ginger and served with a refreshing orange sorbet and wonton wrappers are sealed around a sweet date filling and laced with honey to name but a few of the tempting treats that follow in this chapter.

Sweet Fruit Wontons

Sweet wontons are served mainly in restaurants and are not often found in a Chinese home. They are very adaptable and may be filled with whole, small fruits or a spicy chopped mixture as here.

Serves 4

INGREDIENTS

12 wonton wrappers
2 tsp cornflour (cornstarch)
6 tsp cold water
oil, for deep-frying

2 tbsp clear honey
selection of fresh fruit (such as kiwi
   fruit, limes, oranges, mango and
   apples), sliced, to serve

FILLING:
175 g/6 oz/1 cup chopped dried,
   stoned (pitted) dates
2 tsp dark brown sugar
$^1/_2$ tsp ground cinnamon

1 To make the filling, mix together the dates, sugar and cinnamon in a bowl.

2 Spread out the wonton wrappers on a chopping board and spoon a little of the filling into the centre of each wrapper.

3 Mix together the cornflour (cornstarch) and water and brush this around the edges of the wrappers.

4 Fold the wrappers over the filling, bringing the edges together, then bring the two corners together, sealing with the cornflour (cornstarch) mixture.

5 Heat the oil for deep-frying in a wok to 180°C/350°F, or until a cube of bread browns in 30 seconds. Fry the wontons, in batches, for 2-3 minutes, until golden. Remove the wontons from the oil with a slotted spoon and leave to drain on absorbent kitchen paper (paper towels).

6 Place the honey in a bowl and stand it in warm water, to soften it slightly. Drizzle the honey over the wontons and serve with a selection of fresh fruit.

COOK'S TIP

Wonton wrappers may be found in Chinese supermarkets. Alternatively, make 1 quantity of the dough used for Shrimp Dumpling Soup (see page 24).

Banana Pastries

These pastries require a little time to prepare, but are well worth the effort.
A sweet banana filling is wrapped in dough and baked.

Serves 4

INGREDIENTS

DOUGH:
450 g/1 lb/4 cups plain (all-purpose)
   flour
60 g/2 oz/4 tbsp lard (shortening)
60 g/2 oz/4 tbsp unsalted butter
125 ml/4 fl oz/$^1/_2$ cup water

FILLING:
2 large bananas
75 g/2$^3/_4$ oz/$^1/_3$ cup finely chopped
   no-need-to-soak dried apricots
pinch of nutmeg

dash of orange juice
1 egg yolk, beaten
icing (confectioner's) sugar, for
   dusting
cream or ice cream, to serve

1 To make the dough, sift the flour into a large mixing bowl. Add the lard (shortening) and butter and rub into the flour with the fingertips until the mixture resembles breadcrumbs. Gradually blend in the water to make a soft dough. Wrap in clear film (plastic wrap) and chill in the refrigerator for 30 minutes.

2 Mash the bananas in a bowl with a fork and stir in the apricots, nutmeg and orange juice, mixing well.

3 Roll the dough out on a lightly floured surface and cut out 16 × 10-cm/4-inch rounds.

4 Spoon a little of the banana filling on to one half of each round and fold the dough over the filling to make semi-circles. Pinch the edges together and seal by pressing with the prongs of a fork.

5 Arrange the pastries on a non-stick baking tray (cookie sheet) and brush them with the beaten egg yolk.

6 Cut a small slit in each pastry and cook in a preheated oven, 180°C/350°F/Gas 4, for about 25 minutes, or until golden brown.

7 Dust with icing (confectioner's) sugar and serve with cream or ice cream.

VARIATION

Use a fruit filling of your choice, such as apple or plum, as an alternative.

Mango Dumplings

*Fresh mango and canned lychees fill these small steamed dumplings,
making a really colourful and tasty treat.*

Serves 4

INGREDIENTS

DOUGH:
2 tsp baking powder
1 tbsp caster (superfine) sugar
150 ml/¹/₄ pint/²/₃ cup water
150 ml/¹/₄ pint/²/₃ cup milk

400 g/14 oz/3¹/₂ cups plain (all-
purpose) flour

FILLING AND SAUCE:
1 small mango

100 g/4 oz can lychees, drained
1 tbsp ground almonds
4 tbsp orange juice
ground cinnamon, for dusting

1 To make the dough, place the baking powder and sugar in a large mixing bowl. Mix the water and milk together and then stir this mixture into the baking powder and sugar mixture until well combined. Gradually stir in the flour to make a soft dough. Set the dough aside in a warm place for about 1 hour.

2 To make the filling, peel the mango and cut the flesh from the stone (pit). Roughly chop the mango flesh; reserve half and set aside for the sauce.

3 Chop the lychees and add to half of the chopped mango, together with the ground almonds. Leave to stand for 20 minutes.

4 Meanwhile, make the sauce. Blend the reserved mango and the orange juice in a food processor until smooth. Press the mixture through a sieve to make a smooth sauce.

5 Divide the dough into 16 equal pieces. Roll each piece out on a lightly floured surface into 7.5-cm/ 3-inch rounds.

6 Spoon a little of the mango and lychee filling on to the centre of each round and fold the dough over the filling to make semi-circles. Pinch the edges together to seal firmly.

7 Place the dumplings on a heatproof plate in a steamer, cover and steam for 20-25 minutes, or until cooked through.

8 Remove the dumplings from the steamer, dust with a little ground cinnamon and serve with the mango sauce.

Honeyed Rice Puddings

These small rice puddings are quite sweet, but have a wonderful flavour because of the combination of ginger, honey and cinnamon.

Serves 4

INGREDIENTS

300 g/10 oz/1¹/₂ cups pudding rice
2 tbsp clear honey, plus extra for
   drizzling
large pinch of ground cinnamon

15 no-need-to-soak dried apricots,
   chopped
3 pieces stem (preserved) ginger,
   drained and chopped

8 whole no-need-to-soak dried
   apricots, to decorate

1 Put the rice in a saucepan and just cover with cold water. Bring to the boil, reduce the heat, cover and cook for 15 minutes, or until the water has been absorbed.

2 Stir the honey and cinnamon into the rice.

3 Grease 4 × 150 ml/¹/₄ pint/ ²/₃ cup ramekin dishes.

4 Blend the apricots and ginger in a food processor to make a paste. Divide the paste into 4 equal portions and shape each into a flat round to fit into the base of the ramekin dishes.

5 Divide half of the rice between the ramekins and place the apricot paste on top.

6 Cover the apricot paste with the remaining rice. Cover the ramekins with greaseproof (wax) paper and foil and steam for 30 minutes, or until set.

7 Remove the ramekins from the steamer and leave to stand for 5 minutes.

8 Turn the puddings out on to warm serving plates and drizzle with clear honey. Decorate with dried apricots and serve.

COOK'S TIP

The puddings may be left to chill in their ramekin dishes in the refrigerator, then turned out and served with ice cream or cream.

Poached Allspice Pears

These pears are moist and delicious after poaching in a sugar and allspice mixture.
They are wonderful served hot or cold.

Serves 4

INGREDIENTS

4 large, ripe pears
300 ml/¹/₂ pint/1¹/₄ cups orange
  juice

2 tsp ground allspice
60 g/2 oz/¹/₃ cup raisins
2 tbsp light brown sugar

grated orange rind, to decorate

1 Using an apple corer, core the pears. Using a sharp knife, peel the pears and cut them in half.

2 Place the pear halves in a large saucepan.

3 Add the orange juice, allspice, raisins and sugar to the pan and heat gently, stirring, until the sugar has dissolved. Bring the mixture to the boil for 1 minute.

4 Reduce the heat to low and leave to simmer for about 10 minutes, or until the pears are cooked, but still fairly firm – test

them by inserting the tip of a sharp knife.

5 Remove the pears from the pan with a slotted spoon and transfer to serving plates. Decorate and serve hot with the syrup.

COOK'S TIP

The Chinese do not usually have desserts to finish off a meal, except at banquets and special occasions. Sweet dishes are usually served in between main meals as snacks, but fruit is refreshing at the end of a big meal.

VARIATION

Use cinnamon instead of the allspice and decorate with cinnamon sticks and fresh mint sprigs, if you prefer.

Chinese Custard Tarts

These small tarts are irresistible – a custard is baked in a rich, sweet pastry.
The tarts may be served warm or cold.

Makes 15

INGREDIENTS

DOUGH:
175 g/6 oz/1^1/$_2$ cups plain (all-
    purpose) flour
3 tbsp caster (superfine) sugar
60 g/2 oz/4 tbsp unsalted butter
25 g/1 oz/2 tbsp lard (shortening)

2 tbsp water

CUSTARD:
2 small eggs, separated
60 g/2 oz/^{1}/$_4$ cup caster (superfine)
    sugar

175 ml/6 fl oz/^{3}/$_4$ cup pint milk
^{1}/$_2$ tsp ground nutmeg, plus extra
    for sprinkling
cream, to serve

1 To make the dough, sift the flour into a bowl. Add the sugar and rub in the butter and lard (shortening) until the mixture resembles breadcrumbs. Add the water and mix to form a firm dough.

2 Transfer the dough to a lightly floured surface and knead for 5 minutes, until smooth. Cover with cling film (plastic wrap) and leave to chill in the refrigerator while you prepare the filling.

3 To make the custard, beat the eggs and sugar together. Gradually add the milk and nutmeg and beat until well combined.

4 Separate the dough into 15 even-sized pieces. Flatten the dough pieces into rounds and press into shallow patty tins (pans).

5 Spoon the custard into the pastry cases (tart shells) and cook in a preheated oven, at 150°C/300°F/Gas 2, for 25-30 minutes.

6 Transfer the tarts to a wire rack, leave to cool slightly, then sprinkle with nutmeg. Serve with cream.

COOK'S TIP

For extra convenience, make the dough in advance, cover and leave to chill in the refrigerator until required.

Ginger Lychees With Orange Sorbet

*This dish is truly delicious! The fresh flavour of the sorbet
perfectly complements the spicy lychees.*

Serves 4

INGREDIENTS

SORBET:
225 g/8 oz/¹/₄ cups caster (superfine)
   sugar
450 ml/³/₄ pint/2 cups cold water
350 g/12 oz can mandarins, in
   natural juice

2 tbsp lemon juice

STUFFED LYCHEES:
425 g/15 oz can lychees, drained
60 g/2 oz stem (preserved) ginger,
   drained and finely chopped

lime zest, cut into diamond shapes,
   to decorate

1 To make the sorbet, place the sugar and water in a saucepan and stir over a low heat until the sugar has dissolved. Bring the mixture to the boil and boil vigorously for 2-3 minutes.

2 Meanwhile, blend the mandarins in a food processor or blender until smooth. Press the blended mandarin mixture through a sieve until smooth. Stir the mandarin sauce into the syrup, together with the lemon juice. Set aside to cool.

3 Pour the mixture into a rigid, plastic container suitable for the freezer and freeze until set, stirring occasionally.

4 Meanwhile, drain the lychees on absorbent kitchen paper (paper towels).

5 Spoon the chopped ginger into the centre of the lychees.

6 Arrange the lychees on serving plates and serve with scoops of orange sorbet.

COOK'S TIP

It is best to leave the sorbet in the refrigerator for 10 minutes, so that it softens slightly, allowing you to scoop it to serve.

Battered Bananas

These bananas are quite irresistible, therefore it may be wise to make double quantities for weak-willed guests!

Serves 4

INGREDIENTS

8 medium bananas
2 tsp lemon juice
75 g/2³/₄ oz/²/₃ cup self-raising flour

75 g/2³/₄ oz/²/₃ cup rice flour
1 tbsp cornflour (cornstarch)
¹/₂ tsp ground cinnamon

250 ml/8 fl oz/1 cup water
4 tbsp light brown sugar
oil, for deep-frying

1 Cut the bananas into chunks and place them in a large mixing bowl.

2 Sprinkle the lemon juice over the bananas to prevent discoloration.

3 Sift the self raising flour, rice flour, cornflour (cornstarch) and cinnamon into a mixing bowl. Gradually stir in the water to make a thin batter.

4 Heat the oil in a preheated wok until almost smoking, then reduce the heat slightly.

5 Place a piece of banana on the end of a fork and carefully dip it into the batter, draining off any excess. Repeat with the remaining banana pieces.

6 Sprinkle the sugar on to a large plate.

7 Carefully place the banana pieces in the oil and cook for 2-3 minutes, until golden. Remove the banana pieces from the oil with a slotted spoon and roll them in the sugar. Transfer to serving bowls and serve immediately with cream or ice cream.

COOK'S TIP

Rice flour can be bought from wholefood shops or from Chinese supermarkets.

Index

Index compiled by Hilary Bird.